THE VEGETARIAN KITCHEN

★ *Nourishing, Healthy & Flavoursome* ★

150

GREAT RECIPES

CONTENTS

INTRODUCTION

Vegetarian food used to have a bad rep. It was time-consuming and too-much-tofu. But times have changed and these days vegetarian is synonymous with fresh, healthy and clean eating. Not only that, but it's also easy to prepare, and offers great diversity in flavours and textures. The only hard part of creating a cookbook with 150 delicious vegetarian recipes is deciding what to leave out!

Not eating meat is considered a healthy choice for lots of good reasons. Vegetarians are thought to live longer and be less vulnerable to heart disease and cancer. It's also well known that avoiding meat is kinder to the planet, helping to reduce greenhouse gas emissions, as well as to the animals involved in factory farming. Eliminating meat, or simply eating a bit less, will help you and our planet to become healthier.

In the soup section of this book, you'll find everything you need create the classic winter warmers like Leek and Potato Soup or Minestrone, or try your hand at something a bit different like Soba Noodle Soup.

Salads are no longer a case of putting a few green leaves on a plate. In this book you'll find a wonderful variety; some light accompaniments, like Green Pea and Feta Salad and others a substantial meal in themselves such as Green Papaya or Quinoa Salad.

We've included a few quinoa recipes in this book and here's why: quinoa is a superfood. It's a complete protein, which means it provides all nine essential amino acids necessary for good health. What's more, it's a nutritional powerhouse, contianing protein, fibre, iron, magnesium, folate and heart-healthy omega 3 fatty acids. Don't miss out on experimenting with the delicious quinoa recipes in this book.

There's a chapter in this book dedicated to tarts, fritattas and pizzas and here you'll find recipes for old favourites such as margherita pizza, but here too is an opportunity to experiment. In this book, you'll find recipes that reinvent pizza with a crust made out of cauliflower, almonds or even slices of eggplant – ideal if you're taking a raincheck on gluten.

There's classic and experimental when it comes to burgers and pasta too. You'll find recipes for lentil burgers, chickpea burgers and beetroot patties. Who doesn't love a comforting pasta bake? You'll find a recipe for that in this book, along with other traditional pasta sauces. And you'll also discover how to make your own beetroot pasta and pumpkin gnocchi from scratch and even how to make pasta noodles from zucchini.

No good cookbook is complete without desserts, and you'll find plenty of recipes for fresh, fruity options as well as the more decadent and chocolatey varieties.

A full chapter is dedicated to vegan meals, those that don't use any animal produce at all. Vegan was perhaps considered marginal, but not any more. It's mainstream and it's easy. You'll find vegan recipes for curry, chocolate cake and tacos. There's no need to miss out if you choose to go vegan.

Let's celebrate vegetables. Vegetables are wholesome, healthy, delicious and downright good for you! You'll find all types in this book, but a special mention is made for kale. Check out the kale slaw or the kale stir fry. Cook one of these for your family tonight and you'll be giving them a motherload of nutrients: Vitamins A, K, C, B1, B2, B3, B6, Manganese, Calcium, Copper, Potassium, Magnesium, Iron and Phosphorus. And it tastes great too! So dive in, experiment with the great recipes in this book, and you'll be happy, healthy and satisfied.

SOUPS
AND
SALADS

CAULIFLOWER CREAM SOUP

INGREDIENTS

2 heads cauliflower,
broken into florets

1 tbsp olive oil

3 cloves garlic,
choppped

½ tsp cumin seeds

2 spring onions,
chopped

3 cups (750ml, 24fl oz)
vegetable stock

1 cup (250ml, 8fl oz)
water

1 tsp dried thyme

1 bay leaf

2 cups (500ml, 1pt)
heavy cream

Salt and pepper, to taste

Fresh parsley, chopped,
and pepper to garnish

METHOD

1. Preheat the oven to 220°C (430°F, Gas Mark 7) and line a baking tray with greaseproof paper.

2. In a large bowl, toss cauliflower pieces with olive oil, garlic, cumin seeds and spring onions. Spread out pieces on baking tray.

3. Place in oven and roast for 30 minutes, until golden and tender.

4. Transfer cauliflower to a soup pot and pour in the vegetable stock and water. Add thyme and bay leaf and bring to a boil. Reduce to a gentle simmer and cover the pot. Cook for 30 minutes. Remove and discard the bay leaf.

5. Transfer to a blender and puree in batches, then return to the pot. Or puree the soup in the pot using an immersion blender, if you have one.

6. Stir in the cream and season with salt and pepper. Heat through, but do not boil, and then serve garnished with chopped parsley and pepper.

SALAD WITH VEGETABLES AND MISO DRESSING

INGREDIENTS

Dressing

1 tbsp miso paste

2 tbsps rice vinegar

1 tbsp honey

1 tbsp ginger, minced

1 tbsp sesame oil

1½ tsp lime juice

1 tsp toasted
sesame seeds

Salad

1 potato, peeled and
cut into pieces

1 small head broccoli,
broken into florets

½ red leaf lettuce

½ butter leaf lettuce

100g (3½oz) labneh
cheese, diced

2 tsp toasted sesame
seeds, to garnish

METHOD

1. In a small bowl, whisk miso paste and rice vinegar together until smooth. Add honey, ginger, sesame oil, lime juice and sesame seeds and mix well to combine.

2. Place the potato in a pan of salted water on a medium-high heat and bring to the boil. Cook for 15 minutes until tender.

3. Remove potato with a slotted spoon. Lower broccoli florets into the water and cook for 5-7 minutes until just tender. Allow to cool slightly.

4. To assemble the salad, place all ingredients in serving bowls and pour the dressing over. Garnish with toasted sesame seeds..

WINTER SALAD WITH ROASTED PECANS

METHOD

1. Preheat the oven to 180°C (350°F, Gas Mark 4).

2. Mix the pecans on a baking sheet with the tsp of olive oil, the salt, and a few grinds of black pepper. Toss the pecans so they're well coated and toast them in the oven for 10 minutes, stirring midway during baking, until lightly toasted. Remove from oven and cool.

3. Place the dressing ingredients into a jar with a secure lid. Shake vigorously. Taste and adjust with oil, vinegar or salt, to taste.

4. Pour dressing into a large serving bowl. Add the torn greens, sliced beetroot and pecans to the bowl and mix gently to coat with dressing.

5. Grind black pepper over the salad and serve.

INGREDIENTS

Salted Pecans

1 cup (185g, 6oz) pecans

1 tsp olive oil

Salt and pepper

Dressing

2 tbsps lemon juice

1 tbsp white wine vinegar

½ tsp sugar

1 tsp garlic, minced

½ cup (125ml, 4fl oz) plain yoghurt

⅓ cup (80ml, 3fl oz) olive oil

Salt and pepper

To serve

160g (6oz) green and red salad leaves

1-2 beetroots, roasted, cooled and thinly sliced

Freshly ground pepper

QUINOA AND APPLE BOWL WITH WALNUT VINAIGRETTE

INGREDIENTS

Walnut vinaigrette

½ cup (100g, 3½oz) roasted walnut oil

1/3 cup (80ml, 3fl oz) balsamic vinegar

1 tbsp maple syrup

2 tsp Dijon mustard

1 clove garlic, minced

1 tsp salt

½ tsp freshly ground pepper

Bowl

1 cup (170g, 6oz) quinoa, rinsed

1 large eggplant, diced

1¾ cups (440ml, 15fl oz) vegetable stock

1/3 cup (40g, 1½oz) walnuts, roughly chopped

¼ cup (30g, 1oz) sunflower seeds

1 apple

1 tsp lemon juice

1/3 cup (50g, 2oz) dried cranberries, roughly chopped or whole

METHOD

1. Place oil, vinegar, maple syrup, mustard, garlic, salt and pepper in a food processor, and pulse until well combined. Set aside until ready to use.

2. Combine quinoa and stock in a medium saucepan. Bring to a boil, then turn heat down to low, cover and simmer for 15 minutes until quinoa is tender. Set aside to cool.

3. Place a medium frying pan over medium high heat. Add eggplant and cook for 10 minutes until soft. Set aside.

4. Wipe pan with kitchen paper. Add walnuts and sunflower seeds and dry fry, stirring constantly, for 1-2 minutes until golden and aromatic.

5. Core and slice the apple and place it in a small bowl. Add lemon juice and toss to cover.

6. In a large mixing bowl combine eggplant, cranberries, apple and quinoa.

7. Before serving toss the dressing through the salad.

LENTIL AND VEGETABLE STEW

INGREDIENTS

2 tbsps olive oil

1 onion, chopped

4 cloves garlic, minced

4 stalks celery, sliced

2 carrots, diced

½ tbsp ground cumin

1 tsp turmeric

1 tsp cinnamon

¼ tsp cayenne pepper

1 x 400g (14oz) can chickpeas, rinsed and drained

2 x 400g (14oz) can diced tomatoes

2 potatoes, diced

6 cups (1.5L, 50fl oz) vegetable stock

1 bay leaf

1 cup (185g, 6oz) brown lentils

Spring onion, sliced, and fresh parsley, to serve

METHOD

1. Heat the oil in a large pot over medium heat until softened. Add onion and garlic and fry for 5 minutes until soft. Add the celery and carrot and sauté for 2 minutes more.

2. Add the cumin, turmeric, cinnamon, and cayenne pepper to the pot. Stir and cook for 1-2 minutes.

3. Add the chickpeas, diced tomatoes and potato. Stir the pot until everything is well mixed.

4. Add the vegetable stock and bay leaf, turn the heat up to high and bring to the boil then add the lentils. Stir and let it come back up to a boil, then turn the heat down to low. Let the stew simmer on low, with the lid on, for 30 minutes until lentils are tender.

5. Remove the bay leaf. Season to taste, then serve garnished with spring onion and parsley.

CARROT GINGER SOUP

INGREDIENTS

1 tbsp olive oil

1 leek, thinly sliced

6 carrots, chopped

Medium piece ginger, grated

3 cups (750ml, 24fl oz) vegetable stock

2 cups (500ml, 1pt) water

Chives and black pepper, to garnish

Crusty bread to serve

METHOD

1. Heat oil in a large saucepan over medium heat. Add leek, carrots and ginger. Fry, stirring occasionally, for 8 minutes, or until vegetables start to soften.

2. Add stock and water to saucepan and bring to the boil. Reduce heat to medium-low and simmer, covered, for 20 minutes, or until carrots are very tender.

3. Remove from heat. Set aside to cool slightly. Transfer to a blender and process in batches, or use an immersion blender in the pot, until smooth.

4. Return to saucepan. Heat over medium heat until hot. Season with salt and pepper.

5. Ladle soup into bowls. Top with chopped chives and fresh black pepper. Serve with crusty bread.

SWEET POTATO AND CARROT SOUP

INGREDIENTS

2 tbsps olive oil

1 onion, chopped

Small piece fresh ginger, finely minced

3 carrots, diced

1-2 sweet potatoes, peeled and diced

3 cups (750ml, 24fl oz) vegetable stock

1 tbsp ground coriander

¼ tsp chilli flakes (optional)

Salt and pepper, to taste

1 garlic clove, very finely grated

Chopped chives, and crusty bread, to serve

METHOD

1. Heat olive oil in a large saucepan over medium high heat. Add onion and fry, stirring, for 5 minutes, or until translucent.

2. Add ginger and cook for 30 seconds. Then add carrots and sweet potatoes and cook for 1-2 minutes, stirring.

3. Add stock and bring to a boil. Reduce heat to low, then add coriander, and chilli flakes (if using) and season with salt and pepper. Cook on a gentle simmer for 20 minutes until carrots and potato are very tender.

4. Turn off heat and allow soup to cool slightly. Add to the blender in batches and puree until smooth, or use an immersion blender in the pot.

5. Return to the pot, add grated garlic and stir. Add water for a thinner consistency.

6. Serve warm, garnished with crusty bread and chopped chives.

EASY THREE BEAN SALAD

INGREDIENTS

Salad

1 x 400g (14oz) can butter beans, drained and rinsed

1 x 400g (14oz) can kidney beans, drained and rinsed

1 x 400g (14oz) can green beans, drained and rinsed

4 spring onions, finely chopped

1 stalk celery, sliced

Dressing

½ cup (100g, 3½oz) apple cider vinegar

¼ cup (60ml, 2fl oz) vegetable oil

1 tbsp honey

½ tsp ground dry mustard

¼ tsp ground black pepper

METHOD

1. In a bowl, gently combine the butter beans, kidney beans, green beans, spring onions, and celery.

2. Place vinegar, oil, honey, mustard and black pepper in a jar with a secure lid and shake vigorously to combine.

3. Pour dressing over the salad, and toss to coat.

4. Cover and refrigerate at least 2 hours,.

5. Remove from fridge and stir to refresh before serving.

FRESH TOMATO SOUP

INGREDIENTS

1¼ kg (3lb 4oz) tomatoes

2 tsps olive oil

3 garlic cloves, minced

3 cups (750ml, 24fl oz)
vegetable stock

¾ tsp salt

2 cups (60g, 2oz)
fresh basil leaves,
thinly sliced

Basil leaves, to serve

METHOD

1. Bring a large saucepan of water to the boil. Drop in tomatoes
   for 1-2 minutes each. Remove and allow to cool before removing
   skins. Set aside.

2. Heat oil in a large saucepan over medium heat. Add garlic
   and cook 30 seconds, stirring constantly. Stir in the stock, salt,
   and tomatoes and bring to a boil. Reduce heat and simmer for 30
   minutes. Stir in basil.

3. Add to the blender in batches and puree until smooth, or use
   an immersion blender in the pot.

4. Garnish with basil leaves to serve.

MINESTRONE SOUP

INGREDIENTS

2 tbsps olive oil

1 onion, chopped

4 carrots, diced

4 celery stalks, chopped

1 zucchini, diced

2 garlic cloves, peeled

100g (3½oz) green beans

1 small head cauliflower, broken into florets

1 cup (135g, 5oz) kale, chopped

3 potatoes, peeled and cubed

1 x 400g (14oz) can chopped tomatoes

3½ cups (875ml, 30fl oz) vegetable stock

1 x 400g (14oz) can cannellini (or butter) beans

Parmesan cheese rind (optional)

Salt and pepper

Grated Parmesan cheese and fresh parsley leaves, to serve

METHOD

1. In a large saucepan, heat the olive oil over medium heat.

2. Add the onion, carrots, celery, zucchini and saute until the vegetables are softened.

3. Grate in the garlic and cook for another 2 minutes, stirring so the garlic doesn't burn.

4 Add the potatoes, kale, cauliflower, green beans and chopped tomatoes, and bring to a simmer.

5. Add the stock, cannellini beans, pepper and Parmesan rind (if using), bring to a simmer and cook for 15 minutes until the potatoes, cauliflower and beans are tender.

6. Season to taste with salt and pepper and and serve hot with freshly grated Parmesan cheese and fresh parsley.

BROCCOLI AND QUINOA SALAD WITH MICROGREENS

INGREDIENTS

1 cup (190g, 7oz) quinoa

2 bunches broccolini,
cut into small florets

2 tbsps olive oil

100g (3½oz) microgreens
(such as purple kohlrabi)

6 radishes, thinly sliced

125g (4oz) goat (or cow)
feta, crumbled

¼ cup (30g, 1oz) pepitas

¼ cup (60ml, 2fl oz)
lemon juice

salt and pepper

METHOD

1. Cook the quinoa according to the directions on the package.

2. Toss the broccolini with the olive oil. Heat a large frying pan on a
    medium high heat. Add the broccolini and cook, turning, for
    5 minutes or until a little bit charred.

3. In a large bowl, combine broccolini with the quinoa, microgreens,
    radishes, feta, pepitas and lemon juice.

4. Season and serve.

WARM ROASTED ZUCCHINI AND CASHEW NUT SALAD

INGREDIENTS

3 zucchini

1 clove garlic, finely chopped

½ cup (60g, 2oz) cashew nuts

Olive oil, for drizzling

½ cup (20g, ¾oz) fresh basil, shredded

½ cup (20g, ¾oz) fresh mint, shredded

2 tbsp olive oil

2 lemons, juiced

Salt and pepper

METHOD

1. Preheat oven to 200°C (400°F, Gas Mark 6).

2. Slice zucchini and arrange in one layer on a baking tray.
    Dot garlic over the zucchini and sprinkle over cashew nuts. Drizzle with oil and season with salt and pepper.

3. Roast for 10 minutes, turning zucchini over half way through, until zucchini is soft and golden.

4. In a shallow dish, gently combine zucchini with herbs, olive oil and the juice of the lemons. Season with salt and pepper.
    Serve warm.

POTATO AND LEEK SOUP WITH CROUTONS

INGREDIENTS

Croutons

30g (1oz) butter

1 small loaf day-old bread, cubed

Soup

3 tbsps butter

4 leeks, white and pale green parts only, roughly sliced

3 cloves garlic, crushed

900g (1 lb) potatoes, peeled and roughly chopped

6 cups (1.5L, 50fl oz) vegetable stock

1 cup (250ml, 8fl oz) water

2 bay leaves

1 sprig fresh thyme

1 tsp salt

¼ tsp black pepper

1 cup (250ml, 8fl oz) thickened cream

METHOD

1. Melt butter in a large frying pan on medium-high heat. Add the bread in one layer on the bottom of the pan. Leave to cook until golden on one side and then turn over with a spatula and brown on the other side. Remove from heat and drain the croutons on paper towels. Set aside.

2. Melt butter over medium heat in a large saucepan. Add leeks and garlic and fry, stirring regularly, for 10 minutes until soft but not brown. Adjust heat if required.

3. Add potatoes, stock, water, bay leaves, thyme, salt and pepper to pot and bring to a boil. Cover and turn the heat down to low. Simmer for 20 minutes, or until the potatoes are very soft.

4. Remove thyme sprig and bay leaves. Purée the soup in the pot with immersion blender, or allow to cool slightly and then puree in batches with an upright blender, until smooth.

5. Add cream and bring to a simmer. Season to taste with salt and pepper. Simmer, uncovered, to thicken or add more water or stock for a thinner consistency. Garnish with croutons.

BROCCOLI HERB SALAD

INGREDIENTS

1 broccoli head, broken into small florets

2 avocados

1 cucumber

1 butter lettuce

Handful parsley, chopped

Handful dill, chopped

½ lemon, quartered, to serve

METHOD

1. Bring a medium pan of water to the boil. Add broccoli and boil for 5 minutes until tender, but crunchy. Set aside to cool slightly.

2. Slice cucumber and avocados vertically.

3. Assemble the salad by placing lettuce leaves on a plate and arrange the avocado and cucumber on top. Garnish with parsley and dill and lemon quarters.

4. Drizzle salad with lemon coriander dressing (opposite).

LEMON PARSLEY DRESSING

INGREDIENTS

1 bunch fresh parsley, leaves picked, chopped

1½ lemons, juiced and zested

1 tbsp tahini

2 tbsps olive oil

1 tsp tamari (or soy sauce)

1 tsp honey

METHOD

1. Place all dressing ingredients into a medium jar with a secure lid and shake vigorously to combine.

SERVES 6 ★ PREP 20MIN ★ COOK TIME 1HR 15MIN

RIBOLLITA TUSCAN SOUP

INGREDIENTS

Olive oil, for frying

3 garlic cloves, minced

1 onion, roughly chopped

1 carrot, sliced

1 celery stalk, chopped

2 cups (500ml, 1pt) vegetable stock

3 x 400g (14oz) cans cannellini beans, drained and rinsed

3 medium roma or vine tomatoes

1 leek, sliced

1 sprig fresh rosemary, leaves picked

1 bunch kale leaves, roughly chopped

3 thick slices crusty bread (stale)

Olive oil, balsamic vinegar and grated Parmesan, to serve

METHOD

1. Heat the oil in a large pot over medium heat. Add garlic, onion, carrot and celery and fry for 5 minutes, until soft.
2. Pour in stock and then add beans, tomatoes, leek and rosemary. Simmer, covered, for about an hour until the beans and vegetables are very tender.
3. Add the kale and bread and cook for 5 minutes more.
4. To serve, drizzle with olive oil and balsamic vinegar and sprinkle over the Parmesan cheese.

EDAMAME AND COCONUT QUINOA SALAD

INGREDIENTS

Dressing

2 limes, juiced

½ tsp salt

½ tsp black pepper

1 garlic clove, minced

¼ cup (10g, ¼ oz) fresh coriander, finely chopped

¼ cup (60ml, 2fl oz) extra-virgin olive oil

½ tsp ground cumin

Salad

1 cup (190g, 7oz) red quinoa

200g edamame pods (fresh or frozen)

1 cup (90g, 3oz) coconut flakes

½ cup (80g, 3oz) raisins

½ red capsicum, finely diced

½ yellow capsicum, finely diced

METHOD

1. Place the ingredients for the dressing into a jar with a secure lid and shake vigorously to combime.

2. Cook quinoa according to the instructions on the packet. Set aside to cool.

3. Bring a pot of lightly salted water to the boil in a medium saucepan. Add the edamame pods and return the water to boiling. Boil pods for 5 minutes. Drain.

4. Place cooled quinoa in a large bowl and fluff with a fork. Add the edamame, coconut flakes, raisins and red and yellow capsicum and mix to combine.

5. Drizzle dressing over salad and toss well. Season to taste before serving.

SERVES 4 ★ PREP 20MIN

SOUTHWESTERN BLACK BEAN SALAD

INGREDIENTS

2 cups (340g, 12oz) sweet corn kernels, frozen or fresh

1 x 400g (14 oz) can black beans, drained and rinsed

1 large cucumber, diced

1 large red capsicum, diced

15 cherry tomatoes, halved

4 spring onions, sliced

1/3 cup (10g, ¼oz) parsely leaves, chopped

Dressing

2 tbsps olive oil

2 limes, juiced

2 tbsps ground cumin

1 tsp Tabasco sauce (or other hot sauce)

METHOD

1. In a large bowl, mix together corn, black beans, cucumber, capsicum, cherry tomatoes, spring onions and parsley.

2. In a small bowl or sealed jar, combine all ingredients for the dressing.

3. Place salad and dressing in a large bowl and toss well to combine.

MEXICAN CORN SALAD WITH LIME VINAIGRETTE

INGREDIENTS

5 corn cobs

2 tbsps olive oil

100g (3½ oz) feta cheese

½ cup (15g, ½ oz) fresh coriander, chopped

2 tbsps red onion, finely chopped

2 garlic cloves, minced

1 tbsp jalapeno peppers, finely chopped

Salt and pepper

Lime vinaigrette

2 tbsp lime juice

½ tsp honey

¼ tsp cayenne pepper

½ tsp chilli powder

¼ cup (60ml, 2fl oz) extra-virgin olive oil

Fresh coriander, chopped, to garnish

METHOD

1. Brush the corn cobs with olive oil. Place cobs in a large frying pan over medium high heat and cook, turning frequently, for 10 minutes or until corn is nicely charred. Remove from heat and set aside. When cool, slice kernels off the cob.

2. Meanwhile, combine feta cheese, coriander, red onion, garlic, jalapenos, and salt and pepper in a large bowl. Gently mix the corn kernels into the bowl.

3. In a small bowl mix together lime juice, honey, cayenne pepper, and chilli and then slowly drizzle in the olive oil, whisking until emulsified. Season to taste.

4. Pour dressing over salad and toss to combine. Garnish with fresh coriander to serve.

BAKED NEW POTATO SALAD

INGREDIENTS

750g (1½ lb) whole
new potatoes

1 tbsp olive oil

455g (1lb) mixed mushrooms

6 garlic cloves,
skins on

½ pumpkin, cut into
bite-sized pieces

1 cup (125g, 4oz) mozzarella
cheese

Salt and pepper,
to taste

Spring onion, sliced,
and fresh dill, to garnish

METHOD

1. Preheat oven to 235°C (455°F, Gas Mark 8).

2. Toss potatoes and olive oil and place in an ovenproof roasting dish.
   Transfer to the oven and roast uncovered for 15 minutes.

3. Remove from oven and stir in mushrooms, garlic and pumpkin.
   Sprinkle cheese over the top. Return to the oven to roast for another
   25 minutes or until everything is caramelised and golden brown,
   and cheese has melted.

4. Season to taste with salt and pepper and serve garnished
   with fresh herbs and spring onion slices.

BUTTERNUT SAGE SOUP

INGREDIENTS

2 tbsps olive oil

1 carrot, diced

1 celery stalk, diced

1 onion, diced

1 small butternut pumpkin, diced

2 tsps chopped fresh sage

4 cups (1L, 2pt) vegetable stock

½ tsp salt

½ tsp pepper

Pepitas and sage, to garnish

METHOD

1. Heat oil in a large saucepan. Add carrot, celery and onion and cook, stirring, for 5 minutes or until vegetables have begun to soften and the onion turns translucent.

2. Add butternut pumpkin, sage, vegetable stock, salt and pepper. Bring to a boil, reduce heat and simmer for 30 minutes, or until pumpkin is very tender.

3. Use an immersion blender in the pot to purée soup or, cool slightly and purée in batches in an upright blender.

4. Serve hot and garnished with pepitas and sage leaves.

WALNUT, GOAT'S CHEESE AND ROASTED BEET SALAD

INGREDIENTS

Dressing

5 tbsps olive oil

3 tbsps white wine vinegar

¼ tsp sea salt

¼ tsp sugar (optional)

Salad

¾ cup (90g, 3oz) walnuts, coarsely chopped, toasted

550g (1¼ lb) beetroots

1-2 baby cos lettuce, shredded

1 small cucumber, sliced

15-20 red and yellow cherry tomatoes

80g (3oz) soft goat's cheese, cut into pieces

METHOD

1. Preheat oven to 200°C (400°F, Gas Mark 6).

2. To prepare dressing, place all dressing ingredients in a small jar with a secure lid and shake well to combine. Refrigerate until ready to serve.

3. Heat a large saucepan over medium high heat. Add walnuts and dry fry, stirring, for 3-4 minutes, or until nicely browned.

4. Rinse beets and cut off tops. Place on a baking tray and cook for 50 minutes, or until beets are tender when pierced with a sharp knife. Remove from oven and allow to cool before removing skins. Slice beets as desired.

5. Place lettuce, cucumber and tomatoes in a large shallow bowl and toss with half the dressing. Place beetroot, walnuts and goat's cheese on top and drizzle over the remaining dressing.

HEARTY BEAN SOUP

INGREDIENTS

1 tsp vegetable oil

1 onion, chopped

2 garlic cloves, minced

2 carrots, diced

1 tsp salt

2 cups (500ml, 1pt)
vegetable stock

1½ cups (375ml,
13fl oz) water

2 potatoes, peeled
and diced

2 tbsps tomato paste

1 tsp chilli powder
(optional)

1 tsp ground cumin

1 tsp dried mixed herbs

1 x 400g (14oz) can
kidney beans, drained
and rinsed

Salt and pepper, to
season

METHOD

1. Heat oil in a large saucepan over medium-high heat. Cook onion, garlic, carrots and salt, stirring occasionally, for 5 minutes, or until vegetables are tender.

2. Pour stock and water into the pan, and bring to a boil. Add potatoes and tomato paste. Return to a boil. Stir in chilli powder, if using, cumin and herbs.

3. Reduce heat to low and cook on a gentle simmer, covered, for 20 minutes, or until potatoes are cooked.

4. Stir in kidney beans, and return to a boil.

5. Season to taste with salt and pepper before serving.

SERVES 2 ★ PREP 35MIN

GREEN PAPAYA SALAD

INGREDIENTS

1 small green papaya

3 carrots, julienned

90g (3oz) green cabbage, grated (optional)

100g (3½oz) green beans, trimmed and halved

2 beef tomatoes, sliced

1-2 large red chillis, halved lengthways

100g (3½oz) bean sprouts

¾ cup (90g, 3oz) roasted peanuts (reserve some for garnish)

Sauce

2 cloves garlic, minced

2 tbsp roasted peanuts

2 bird's eye chillies

1 tbsp coconut sugar

¼ tsp salt

2 limes, juiced

2 tbsps vegan fish sauce

METHOD

1. Peel the skin off the papaya using a vegetable peeler, then halve lengthwise and scoop out seeds. Grate or julienne the papaya pieces.

2. Add papaya, carrots, cabbage, if using, beans, and tomatoes to a large mixing bowl.

3. For the sauce, place garlic, peanuts, chillies, coconut sugar and salt in a food processor and pulse until a fine paste forms.

4. Transfer paste to a small mixing bowl. Add lime juice and vegan fish sauce. Whisk to combine. Taste and adjust seasonings as required.

5. Pour sauce over vegetables. Add chillis, bean sprouts and peanuts and toss to combine.

6. Garnish with extra peanuts to serve.

RED AND WHITE RICE BOWL

INGREDIENTS

Dressing

6 tbsps olive oil

2 tbsps white wine vinegar

1 lime, juiced

1½ tsp coriander seeds, lightly crushed

1 tsp Dijon mustard

Pinch of sugar

Salt and pepper

Salad

200g (7oz) red rice

200g (7oz) basmati rice

1 head broccoli, broken into florets

1 x 400g (14oz) can chickpeas, drained and rinsed

½ bunch coriander, finely chopped

½ bunch flat leaf parsley, finely chopped

½ cup (60g, 2oz) almonds, halved

METHOD

1. Place all the dressing ingredients in a small bowl or jug and mix well. Taste and adjust the seasoning as required.

2. Cook rices separately according to pack instructions until tender. Drain well and transfer to a serving bowl.

3. Bring a medium pan of water to the boil. Add broccoli and boil for 5 minutes until tender, but crunchy. Set aside to cool slightly.

4. Add chickpeas, herbs and almonds to the warm rice and mix well.

5. Pour dressing over the rice salad and toss together. Top with broccoli to serve.

GREEN PEA AND FETA SALAD

INGREDIENTS

Dressing

½ tsp Dijon mustard

1 tbsp lemon juice

3 tbsps olive oil

Pinch of sugar

Salad

200g (7oz) green beans, topped and tailed

175g (6oz) raw peas, podded

½ red onion, thinly sliced

60g baby beet leaves (or baby spinach)

125g (4oz) feta cheese, cubed

Salt and pepper, to season

METHOD

1. To prepare dressing, place mustard, lemon juice, oil and sugar into a jar with a secure lid and shake vigorously to combine. Season to taste.

2. Bring a pan of water to the boil. Add the green beans and cook for 5 minutes, or until the beans are just tender. Drain and refresh the beans under cold water.

3. Put the beans into a large serving bowl. Add the raw peas, red onion, baby beet leaves and feta cheese. Pour over dressing and and toss gently to combine.

4. Season to taste before serving.

CARROT AND KALE SLAW

INGREDIENTS

1 small purple cabbage, finely shredded

1 carrot, julienned

1 bunch kale leaves, thick stems removed, roughly chopped

$1/3$ cup (60g, 2oz) sunflower seeds

Dressing

¼ cup (60ml, 2fl oz) Dijon mustard

1 orange, juiced

¼ cup (60ml, 2fl oz) balsamic vinegar

½ tsp black pepper

METHOD

1. Combine cabbage, carrot, kale and sunflower seeds in a serving bowl.

2. In a small bowl, whisk together mustard, orange juice, vinegar and pepper.

3. Pour dressing over salad and toss to coat.

CREAMY BROCCOLI SOUP

INGREDIENTS

450g (1lb) broccoli

60g (2oz) butter

1 onion, chopped

¼ cup (30g, oz) plain flour

4 cups (1L, 2pt) vegetable stock

¼ cup (60ml, 2fl oz) heavy cream

Salt and pepper

4 broccoli florets, steamed, linseed and microgreens, to garnish

METHOD

1. Prepare the broccoli by cutting into florets, and peeling and chopping the stems.

2. In a large saucepan, melt butter over medium heat. Add onion and fry, stirring occasionally, for 5 minutes or until softened.

3. Add flour and cook, stirring, for 1 minute until combined. Over high heat add stock and 1 cup water and, whisking constantly, bring to a boil. Reduce heat and simmer, whisking occasionally, for 10 minutes.

4. Add broccoli and cook for 15 minutes or until broccoli is very tender.

5. Transfer mixture to a large bowl. In batches, fill a blender halfway with mixture and puree until smooth. If heat builds up, remove cap from blender and cover with a clean teatowel. Return soup to pot when pureed.

6. Add cream and heat over medium heat until warmed through. Season with salt and pepper. Thin with stock or water, if desired.

7. Serve garnished with broccoli florets, linseeds and microgreens.

SOBA NOODLE SOUP

INGREDIENTS

100g (3½ oz) soba
noodles

1 tsp yellow or red miso

3 cups (750ml, 24fl oz)
water

2 tsps soy sauce

2 thin slices ginger,
peeled and cut into
matchsticks

1 clove garlic, thinly
sliced

3 shiitake mushrooms,
wiped, stems removed
and sliced

1 spring onion, thinly
sliced, plus extra for
garnish

½ cup (125g, 4oz)
medium tofu,
diced (optional)

1 tsp ponzu sauce

METHOD

1. Cook the soba noodles according to the instructions on the packet. Drain. If using buckwheat noodles, rinse with cold water to remove excess starch.

2. Meanwhile, in a small bowl, whisk together the miso and ½ cup water.

3. In a medium-size saucepan, bring the remaining 2½ cups water, soy sauce, ginger, and garlic to a boil. Reduce the heat and simmer for 10 minutes.

4. Add the shiitakes, spring onions, and tofu (if using), and simmer for 2 to 3 minutes. Gently stir in the miso and ponzu sauce.

5. Ladle into bowls and garnish with extra spring onions.

WINTER SOUP

INGREDIENTS

2 tbsps olive oil

2 leeks, white and pale-green parts only, halved lengthwise, sliced

2 celery stalks, sliced

1 medium carrot, diced

2 garlic cloves, minced

Pinch of red pepper flakes (optional)

1 tsp salt

3 cups (750ml, 24fl oz) vegetable stock

1½ cups (375ml, 13fl oz) water

1 small butternut pumpkin, finely cubed

1 potato, finely diced

2 tbsps lemon juice

Salt and pepper, to taste

2 tbsps thyme

METHOD

1. Heat oil in a large saucepan over medium-high heat. Cook leeks, celery, carrot, garlic, red-pepper flakes (if using), and salt, stirring occasionally, for 5 minutes, or until leeks are translucent and vegetables are tender.

2. Pour stock and water into the pan, and bring to a boil. Add pumpkin and potato. Return to a boil.

3. Reduce heat to low and cook on a gentle simmer, covered, for 20 minutes, or until vegetables are tender.

4. Stir in lemon juice and herbs. Season to taste with salt and pepper before serving garnished with fresh thyme.

SAVOY CABBAGE AND CHICKPEA SALAD

INGREDIENTS

115g (4oz) chickpeas

1 bay leaf

1 garlic clove, bashed

1 tbsp olive oil

½ small savoy cabbage, tough stalk removed, leaves roughly chopped

2 avocados

Dressing

½ lemon, juiced

3 tbsps extra-virgin olive oil

1 tsp hot mustard

½ tsp sugar

Salt and pepper, to taste

Lemon slices and fresh parsley, to garnish

METHOD

1. Place chickpeas into a saucepan and cover with cold water. Bring pan to the boil for 1 minute and then remove from heat and drain. Return chickpeas to the pan and cover with water to a level about 1cm above the peas. Add the bay leaf and garlic and bring back up to a very gentle simmer. Cover and cook for 25 minutes, until chickpeas are tender but not mushy.

2. Whisk together all the dressing ingredients in a small bowl. Set aside.

3. Drain the chickpeas and discard bay leaf and garlic. Toss with two tbsps of the dressing, and set aside to cool completely.

4. Bring a pan of salted water to a boil. Add cabbage and cook for 30 seconds. Drain and then rinse under a cold tap to refresh. Leave to drain in the colander or dry in a salad spinner.

5. Peel and chop the avocados and mix with the chickpeas and cabbage. Pour over half the dressing and toss to coat.

6. Divide between four plates, trickle over the remaining dressing and serve, garnished with lemon slices and fresh parsley.

TARTS, PIZZA AND FRITTERS

LEEK AND ZUCCHINI TART

SERVES 6 ★ PREP 40min (PLUS CHILLING) ★ COOK TIME 45min

INGREDIENTS

Pastry

1¼ cup (155g, 5oz) plain flour

¼ tsp salt

8 tbsps cold butter, chopped

4 tbsps very cold water

Filling

2 zucchini, sliced, plus ½ zucchini, very thinly sliced on the round

½ tsp salt

1 tsp olive oil

1 tbsp butter

3-4 leeks, chopped, white part only

½ bunch dill leaves, chopped

Pinch of salt

1 cup (250ml, 8fl oz) thickened cream

2 eggs, beaten

¼ tsp pepper

½ cup (60g, 2oz) cheddar or Swiss cheese, grated

Dill, to garnish

METHOD

1. Combine flour and salt in a large bowl. Add butter and rub with fingertips until it resembles coarse crumbs. Gradually add water, until the mixture begins to hold together. Gather dough into a ball and flatten into a thick disk. Wrap in plastic wrap and refrigerate for 30 minutes.

2. Pre-heat oven to 220°C (425°F, Gas Mark 7) and grease 6 springform tartlet pans and one baking tray.

3. Turn pastry onto a floured surface and roll into a circle. Press pastry into tartlet tins and trim edges. Prick bottom of pastry shell with fork. Line the pastry with baking paper, and fill with dried beans, then place in the oven and blind bake for 20 minutes. Remove beans and paper and return to oven to bake for a further 10 minutes. Remove from oven and cool completely on wire rack.

4. Arrange zucchini slices on prepared sheet in a single layer. Sprinkle with salt and drizzle with oilve oil. Bake for 10 minutes, until softened and starting to brown.

5. Melt butter in a large skillet over medium heat. Add leeks, dill leaves and a pinch of salt. Cover and cook over medium-low heat for 5 minutes, until leeks have softened. Set aside 6 slices of leek to finish.

6. Combine cream, eggs, leeks and pepper in a medium bowl. Pour mixture into crust. Arrange overlapping thin slices of zucchini on top of cream mixture and sprinkle cheese on top. Finish each tartlet with one slice of leek and a sprig of dill.

7. Place in the oven and bake for 30 minutes, until filling is set and cheese is golden on top. Cool on a wire rack.

ASPARAGUS PIZZA WITH CAULIFLOWER CRUST

INGREDIENTS

Crust

1 head cauliflower, cut into chunks

100g (3½ oz) ground almonds

2 eggs, beaten

1 tbsp dried mixed herbs

½ tsp salt

¼ tsp pepper

Tomato sauce

1 x 225g (8oz) can tomato paste

2 tbsp olive oil

2 cloves garlic, minced

¼ tsp salt

Pinch of pepper

Topping

1-2 zucchini, very thinly sliced

Asparagus spears, grilled or steamed

3 tbsps basil pesto

Fresh basil leaves and microgreens, to garnish

METHOD

1. Preheat the oven to 220°C (425°F, Gas Mark 7). Line a baking tray with baking paper and brush with oil.

2. Place half the cauliflower in a food processor and pulse until finely chopped and appearing like rice. Transfer to a bowl and repeat with the remaining half.

3. Cover the bowl with plastic wrap and microwave on high for 5 minutes until softened. Tip onto a clean tea towel and allow to cool slightly. Squeeze as much liquid as you can out of the cauliflower by wringing the tea towel over the sink. Transfer to a clean bowl. Add the ground almonds, egg, mixed herbs and salt and pepper and mix well to combine.

4 Scoop the cauliflower mix into the centre of the tray, then press out into a round. Create a slightly thicker crust at the edges. Transfer to the oven and bake for 15 minutes or until golden brown at the edges.

5. Place the ingredients for the tomato sauce in a bowl and stir to combine. Set aside.

6. Remove pizza crust from oven and add toppings. Smear tomato paste on the entire base, then add zucchini slices to cover. Place asparagus spears on top and then drizzle the pesto over. Return to the oven another 5 minutes to heat through.

7. Remove from the oven and serves, garnished with fresh basil and microgreens.

MUSHROOM THYME FRITTATA

INGREDIENTS

Olive oil, for frying

220g (8oz) mixed mushrooms, sliced

½ cup (60g, 2oz) Parmesan cheese, grated

1½ tsps fresh thyme, chopped (or 1tsp dried thyme)

¼ tsp black pepper

⅛ tsp salt

3 egg whites

2 eggs

2 spring onions, sliced, to garnish (optional)

METHOD

1. Preheat grill on a medium setting.

2. Heat oil in a large frying pan over medium-high heat. Add mushrooms to pan and saute for 10 minutes until tender and lightly browned.

3. Place mushrooms in a medium-sized mixing bowl and allow to cool slightly. Wipe frying pan clean.

4. Combine mushrooms, cheese, thyme, black pepper, salt, egg whites, and eggs in a medium bowl and stir until well combined.

5. Heat oil in the same frying pan over medium heat. Add mushroom mixture and cook, covered, for 3 minutes or until almost set.

6. Remove from heat and place under grill for 2 minutes or until egg is set.

7. Serve garnished with spring onion, if using.

SPINACH AND FETA QUICHE

INGREDIENTS

100g (3½ oz) butter

½ cup (125ml, 4fl oz) milk

1 cup (125g, 4oz) plain flour, sifted

1 cup (250ml, 8fl oz) cream

4 eggs

220g (8oz) feta, crumbled

150g (5oz) baby spinach, chopped

½ tsp salt

¼ tsp pepper

METHOD

1. Preheat oven to 200°C (400°F, Gas Mark 6) and grease a 23cm (9in) quiche dish.

2. Heat butter and milk in a medium saucepan over a low heat, stirring until butter is melted. Add flour and whisk until mixture comes together. Remove from heat and allow to cool slightly. Roll dough out on a board. Ease into prepared dish.

3. Line the pastry with baking paper, and fill with dried beans, then place in the oven and blind bake for 10 minutes. Remove beans and paper and return to oven to bake for a further 5 minutes. Cool slightly. Reduce oven to 180°C (350°F, Gas Mark 4).

4 Combine cream, eggs, feta and spinach in a mixing bowl. Add salt and pepper. Pour into pastry in dish.

5. Place in the oven and bake for 50 minutes, until quiche is set and pastry is golden brown.

SERVES 6 ★ PREP 15MIN ★ COOK TIME 1HR 10MIN

MUSHROOM SAGE TART

INGREDIENTS

3 tbsps olive oil

2 red onions, sliced

300g (10oz) mushrooms, sliced

1 tsp salt

12 fresh sage leaves, chopped

3 tbsps balsamic vinegar

1 sheet frozen puff pastry, defrosted but still cool

2 tbsps macadamia nuts, finely chopped, to garnish

1 spring onion, sliced, to garnish

METHOD

1. Preheat the oven to 180°C (350°F, Gas Mark 4).

2. Heat the olive oil in a large frying pan over medium heat. Add the onions and cook, stirring, for 8 minutes until softened.

3. Add the mushrooms and salt and continue cooking until the pan starts to dry out. Then add the sage and the balsamic vinegar and reduce the heat to medium-low. Cook, stirring occasionally, for 25 minutes until caramelised and golden. Remove from the heat and set aside.

4. Unfold the sheet of puff pastry on a baking tray lined with greaseproof paper. Spread the onion, mushroom and sage mixture evenly over the top.

5. Bake the tart in the centre of the oven for 30 minutes, until the pastry is golden brown and flaky.

6. Garnish with chopped macadamia nuts and spring onion and serve warm.

BEETROOT, WALNUT AND GOAT'S CHEESE TART

INGREDIENTS

500g (1lb 2oz) puff pastry

4 tbsps olive oil

3 red onions, finely sliced

2 tbsps balsamic vinegar

Salt and pepper, to season

1 sprig rosemary, leaves picked and chopped (optional)

350g (12oz) cooked beetroot, finely chopped

200g (7oz) soft goat cheese

Olive oil, for drizzling

2 tbsps walnuts, roughly chopped

Baby beetroot leaves, to garnish

METHOD

1. Preheat the oven to 190°C (375°F, Gas Mark 5) and flour a baking tray.

2. On a lightly floured surface, roll the pastry into a rectangle.

3. Place pastry on baking sheet and prick with a fork. Transfer to the oven to bake for 20 minutes.

4. Heat the oil in a large saucepan over a medium-high heat. Add the onions and fry for 2 minutes, stirring constantly. Add balsamic vinegar, a tablespoon of water and salt and pepper. Cover the pan and reduce heat to very low. Leave the onions to sweat for 20 minutes, stirring ocassionally, until completely soft.

5. Add the rosemary, if using, and beetroot and stir to combine. Increase heat if mixture needs to be further reduced. Mixture should be firm.

6. Spread a thin layer of the goat's cheese on the base of the pastry and then top with the onion and beetroot mixture. Drizzle with olive oil.

7. Return tart to the oven to cook for a further 10 minutes. Remove and scatter walnuts over the top. Return to the oven for 5 minutes.

8. Serve immediately, garnished with spinach leaves.

CABBAGE AND SPINACH FRITTERS

INGREDIENTS

Dipping Sauce

1 small clove garlic, finely minced

200g (7oz) plain Greek yoghurt

Salt and pepper, to taste

Fritters

½ small cabbage, shredded

3 spring onions, sliced

2 heads spinach, leaves picked and chopped

2 tbsps coconut flour

4 eggs

1 tbsp soy sauce

¼ tsp pepper

Coconut oil or olive oil, for frying

METHOD

1. Combine garlic and yoghurt in a small bowl. Season to taste. Set aside.

2. In a large mixing bowl, mix together the cabbage, spring onions, spinach and coconut flour.

3. In a small bowl, whisk together eggs, soy sauce and pepper.

4. Stir the egg mixture into the cabbage mixture and mix well to combine.

5. Heat oil in a large frying pan over medium high heat. Drop a heaped tbsp of batter into the pan for each fritter. Flatten with a spatula and cook for 2 minutes until golden brown. Flip and cook on the other side for a further 2 minutes. Cook in batches if required.

TOMATO, BASIL AND GOAT'S CHEESE TART

INGREDIENTS

1 sheet frozen puff pastry

2 eggs, beaten

1 cup (250ml, 8fl oz) thickened cream

½ cup (15g, ½ oz) basil, chopped

¼ tsp pepper

1 zucchini, very thinly sliced

8-10 cherry tomatoes, halved

100g (3½oz) soft goat's cheese

Basil leaves, to garnish

METHOD

1. Preheat oven to 200°C (400°F, Gas Mark 6).

2. Roll out the puff pastry and shape into a circle about ½ cm thick and place onto a baking tray lined with baking paper. To make the crust, score a border 1cm in from the edge with a sharp knife.

3. Prick bottom of pastry shell with fork. Line the pastry with baking paper, and fill with dried beans, then place in the oven and blind bake for 10 minutes.

4. Combine the egg, cream, basil leaves and pepper in a mixing bowl. Pour mixture into pastry base and arrange zucchini and tomatoes on top. Bake for another 20 minutes until the pastry is golden.

5. Remove from oven and set aside to cool. Crumble goat's cheese on top and garnish with basil leaves to serve.

MINI MARGHERITA PIZZA

INGREDIENTS

Pizza bases

2 cups (250g, 8oz) baker's (or plain) flour

7g (¼ oz) sachet dry active yeast

1 tsp caster sugar

1 tsp salt

¾ cup (200ml, 7fl oz) warm water

1 tbsp olive oil, plus extra to grease

Toppings

Olive oil, to drizzle

½ cup (60g, 2oz) mozzarella cheese, grated

1 beef tomato, thinly sliced

Fresh parsley, to garnish

METHOD

1. Sift flour into a large mixing bowl. Stir in yeast, sugar and salt. Make a well in the centre and pour in water and oil. Bring the dough together with your hands, then turn out onto a lightly floured surface. Clean the bowl for reuse.

2. Knead for 5 minutes by hand (or in an electric mixer with a dough hook) until the dough is smooth.

3. Lightly grease the cleaned bowl with a little oil, then add dough and cover with a tea towel or plastic wrap. Set aside in a warm place to prove for 1 hour, until doubled in size.

4. Preheat oven to 240°C (465°F, Gas Mark 9). Lightly flour two baking trays.

5. Knock back the dough by punching it to remove air and divide into 2 balls. Roll dough out on a lightly floured surface to create 2 very thin, 25cm-diameter bases. Transfer to prepared baking sheets.

6. Drizzle olive oil on the pizza base. Scatter with mozzarella cheese and tomato. Place in the oven and and bake for 10 minutes until cheese has melted and the pizza bases are crisp and golden around the edges.

7. Drizzle the pizzas with a little more olive oil, garnish with parsley then serve immediately.

BROCCOLI CHEESE STICKS

INGREDIENTS

400g (14oz) broccoli florets

1 egg

1 egg white

3 spring onions, finely chopped

1 cup (125g, 4oz) cheddar cheese, grated

¾ cup (90g, 3oz) breadcrumbs

Salt and pepper, to taste

METHOD

1. Preheat oven to 200°C (400°F, Gas Mark 6) and grease a baking tray.

2. Blanch broccoli florets in a pot of boiling water for 1 minute. Finely chop and set aside.

3. In a medium bowl, combine all of the ingredients and season with salt and pepper.

4. Spoon a heaped tablespoon of mixture in your hands and roll into an oval. Repeat with remaining mixture. Place sticks on baking tray.

5. Place in the oven and bake for 20 minutes, turning halfway through cooking, until golden.

6. Serve with tomato sauce (opposite).

SERVES 4 ★ PREP 10MIN ★ COOK TIME 2HR 5MIN

HOMEMADE TOMATO SAUCE

INGREDIENTS

10 ripe tomatoes

2 tbsps olive oil

2 tbsps butter

1 onion, chopped

3 cloves garlic, minced

¼ cup (10g, ¼ oz)
fresh basil, chopped

¼ tsp mixed dried herbs

¼ cup (60ml, 2fl oz)
red wine

1 bay leaf

2 celery ribs

3 tbsps tomato paste

Water, if required

METHOD

1. Bring a pot of salted water to the boil over a medium high heat. Have ready a large bowl of iced water.

2. Plunge whole tomatoes into boiling water for 1 minute until skin starts to peel. Remove with a slotted spoon and transfer to ice bath. Set aside until cool enough to handle, then remove peel and squeeze out seeds using your hands. Chop tomatoes with a knife or puree in blender or food processor.

3. Place oil and butter in a large pot over medium high heat. Add onion and garlic and cook, stirring, for 5 minutes, until onion is soft. Add pureed tomatoes, basil, mixed herbs, wine, bay leaf and whole celery ribs.

4. Bring sauce to a boil, then reduce heat to low. Cover and simmer for 2 hours. Stir in tomato paste and simmer for a further 2 hours. Check occasionally and add water to thin, if needed. Discard bay leaf and celery and serve.

FLATBREADS WITH GRILLED EGGPLANT

INGREDIENTS

Flatbread

3 cups (375g, 12oz) plain flour

1 tsp baking powder

1 tsp salt

4 level tbsps Greek yoghurt

2 tbsps olive oil

¾ cup (185ml, 6fl oz) almond milk (or cow's milk)

Filling

2 eggplants, thinly sliced

Salt, for sprinkling

20 cherry tomatoes, halved

1/3 cup (80ml, 3fl oz) olive oil

Handful of dresh dill, leaves picked

1 tbsp black sesame seeds

¼ cup (60ml, 2fl oz) plain yoghurt

METHOD

1. Sift flour, baking powder and salt over a bowl. Make a well in the centre and add the yoghurt, oil and milk. Bring a rough dough together using your hands. Knead for 1 minute until a soft dough forms. Cover bowl with plastic wrap and set aside for 30 minutes.

2. Meanwhile, place eggplant slices in a shallow dish and sprinkle with salt on both sides. Set aside for 30 minutes, then pour off water and use a paper towel to absorb excess.

3. Preheat a grill over medium-high heat. Brush both sides of eggplant slices with oil. Place on grill, and cook for 5 minutes, until soft and slightly charred. Flip eggplant slices, and cook on the other side. At the same time, arrange tomato halves on the grill and cook for 5 minutes, until soft.

4. Lightly flour a work bench. Divide dough in half, then divide each half in 4 pieces. Roll each piece into a ball. Using a rolling pin, form 8 rectangles.

5. Brush a frying pan with olive oil and set over a medium heat. Cook flatbread for 2 minutes on one side. Brush the top lightly with oil and then flip and cook for a further 2 minutes. Repeat with remaining flatbread.

6. To serve, place eggplant and tomato in the centre of a flatbread. Scatter dill, black sesame seeds and yoghurt over the top and fold the two edges over.

MINT AND VEGETABLE TART

INGREDIENTS

6-8 small broccoli florets

1 zucchini, finely sliced

6-8 sheets ready-made filo pastry

50g (2oz) butter, melted

30g (1oz) breadcrumbs

1 tbsp crème fraîche

3-4 asparagus spears

100g (3½oz) feta (or goat's cheese)

Mint and rocket leaves, to garnish

METHOD

1. Preheat your oven to 200°C (400°F, Gas Mark 6) and line a large tart tin with baking paper.

2. Bring a large saucepan of water to the boil and par-cook the broccoli florets and zucchini slices. Do not overcook. Remove from heat and set aside.

3. Unfold the pastry and brush each piece well with butter, then use pastry to line your tart tin, leaving a little pastry hanging over the edges. Sprinkle a thin layer of breadcrumbs between each layer of pastry as you go to keep the pastry crisp. On the final layer, brush with a extra butter and scrunch the edges together to create border.

4. Prick bottom of pastry base with fork. Line with baking paper, fill with dried beans, and then place in the oven and blind bake for 10 minutes.

5. Spread the crème fraîche over the base. Arrange asparagus, broccoli and zucchini slices on top.

6. Bake for another 20 minutes until the pastry is golden brown and the asparagus is tender.

7. To finish, top with cheese and garnish with mint and rocket leaves.

TRUFFLED MUSHROOM PIZZA

INGREDIENTS

1½ tbsps butter

225g (8oz, ½ lb) button mushrooms, thickly sliced

1 tsp truffle oil

Salt and pepper, to taste

1 ball of pizza dough (store-bought or see recipe on page 64)

Extra-virgin olive oil

225g (8oz, ½ lb) mozzarella cheese, grated

1 tsp dried basil

2 tbsp Parmesan cheese, finely grated

Truffle oil, to finish

Fresh basil, to garnish

METHOD

1. Preheat an oven to 250°C (480°F, Gas Mark 9) and grease a pizza pan or baking tray.

2. Warm butter in a large pan over medium-high heat. Add the mushroms and cook, stirring occasionally, for 5 minutes, until tender. During the last minute, stir in truffle oil. Season mushrooms to taste with salt and pepper, then set aside.

3. Stretch pizza dough into a large round. Drizzle with olive oil and salt and spread around the base. Top evenly with mozzarella cheese, dried basil, mushrooms and Parmesan cheese.

4. Transfer pizza to the oven on the lowest rack and cook for 10-15 minutes until golden.

5. Drizzle pizza very lightly with truffle oil and sprinkle with fresh basil before serving.

FETA AND TOMATO PIZZA

INGREDIENTS

Pizza Base

¼ cup (50g, 2oz) chia seeds

¾ cup (185ml, 6fl oz) water

3 tbsps buckwheat flour (gluten free)

1 tsp dried mixed herbs

1 tsp salt

1 tbsp pine nuts, roughly chopped

2 tbsps pepitas, roughly chopped

Topping

2 fresh tomatoes, sliced

½ red capsicum sliced

50g (2oz) feta cheese, crumbled

3-4 button mushrooms, thinly sliced

½ red onion, thinly sliced

Handful of basil leaves, torn

METHOD

1. Preheat oven to 180°C (350°F, Gas Mark 4) and line a baking tray with greaseproof paper.

2. Combine chia seeds, water, buckwheat flour, herbs and salt in a large bowl and mix well. Leave to stand for 15 minutes until the mixture starts to thicken. Add chopped pine nuts and pepitas and stir well.

3. Spread out the base mix on the baking paper and form the dough in a large oval. Flatten to about 1 cm for a firm thin crust.

4. Place in the oven and bake for 20 minutes until base is firm and golden at the edges.

5. Remove from oven. Add tomato, capsicum, feta cheese, mushrooms, onion and basil and return to the oven. Bake for an additional 10 minutes. Remove and cool.

MUSHROOM, FENNEL AND LEEK TART

INGREDIENTS

Olive oil, for frying

1 bulb fennel, trimmed and quartered

2 medium leeks, rinsed and finely sliced

450g (1lb) button mushrooms, chopped

Salt and pepper, to season

6-8 sheets shortcrust pastry

3 eggs

225g (8oz, ½ lb) goat's cheese

Basil leaves, to garnish

METHOD

1. Heat oven to 200°C (400°F, Gas Mark 6) and grease a circular tart tin.

2. Heat oil in a large frying pan over medium heat. Add fennel and leeks and saute for 5 minutes, until just tender but not brown. Transfer to a bowl and set aside.

3. Refresh the frying pan with more oil and add mushrooms. Saute for 5 minutes. Add fennel mixture and saute together for 1 minute. Season with salt and pepper and then remove pan from heat.

4. Unfold pastry onto lightly floured surface and gently roll to fit the size of your time. Fold the pastry over a rolling pin and drape into the tin. Press pastry into the base and around edges tin with your fingers leaving a small overhang.

5. Break an egg into a small bowl and beat lightly. Brush edges of pastry with egg. Fold pastry edges over to make a rim. Brush entire surface with remaining egg and prick pastry base with a fork.

6. Place in the oven and bake for 10 minutes, until pale golden. Remove from oven and set aside to cool.

7. In a mixing bowl combine 2 eggs with goat's cheese and blend until smooth. Add leek-mushroom-fennel mixture and fold to combine.

8. Fill the pastry case with the mixture and transfer to the oven to bake for 7-10 minutes until set and golden on top.

9. Garnish with basil leaves to serve.

POMEGRANATE PIZZA

INGREDIENTS

1 pre-prepared large pizza base (or follow recipe on page 64)

½ cup (60,g, 2oz) cheddar cheese, grated

1 x 125g (4oz) ball fresh mozarella cheese

150g (5oz) rocket or baby spinach leaves (retain a few for garnish)

3 tbsps pomegranate seeds

METHOD

1. Preheat oven 240°C (465°F, Gas Mark 9) and line a baking tray.

2. Place pizza base on baking tray and top with cheddar cheese. Transfer to the oven to cook for 10 minutes, until melted and bubbling at the edges, and crust is golden.

3. Remove from the oven and top with rocket, mozarella cheese, onion and pomegranete seeds.

4. Return to the oven and bake for a further 5-7 minutes until mozarella softens and ingredients are heated through.

5. Top with spinach leaves before serving.

EGGPLANT MINI PIZZAS

INGREDIENTS

Base

1 large eggplant, sliced into rounds

Salt

Olive oil, for brushing

Topping

4 tomatoes, chopped

½ bunch basil, roughly chopped

225g (8oz, ½ lb) mozzarella cheese, grated

Basil leaves, to garnish

METHOD

1. Preheat the oven to 180°C (350°F, Gas Mark 4) and line a baking tray with greaseproof paper.

2. Place the eggplant rounds onto a large plate or clean tea towel.

3. Lightly salt each side of the eggplant rounds. Leave to sit for 20 minutes. Press down on the eggplant slices with the tea towel or kitchen paper to squeeze out some of the water. Brush the slices with olive oil and place onto the baking sheet.

4. Place in the oven and bake for 20 minutes.

5. Remove from the oven and top pizzas with tomato, basil and mozarella. Return to the oven and bake for about 10 minutes, until cooked through. Garnish with extra basil to serve.

CHICKPEA AND SPINACH FRITTERS

INGREDIENTS

Fritters

Vegetable oil, for frying

2 x 400g (14oz) cans chickpeas, drained and rinsed

100g (3½ oz) spinach leaves

¼ onion, roughly chopped

3 garlic cloves, minced

3 tbsps besan flour (or plain)

Handful fresh dill, roughly chopped

¼ tsp ground coriander

1 tsp salt

½ tsp pepper

Yoghurt cucumber sauce

1½ cups (375ml, 13fl oz) plain Greek yoghurt

¼ cup (50g, 2oz) cucumber, finely diced

2 garlic cloves, minced

1 tbsp fresh lemon juice

Salt, to taste

Lemon wedges, to serve

METHOD

1. Place chickpeas, spinach, onion, garlic, flour, dill, coriander, salt and pepper in the bowl of a food processor and pulse to create a smooth batter. Transfer to a mixing bowl.

2. In a medium saucepan, place sufficient oil to just come up the sides of the pan over high heat and heat until oil is shimmering. Reduce heat to medium-high.

3. Shape mixture into a ball with your hands and then flatten it to make a disc. Repeat until all mixture is formed into fritters.

4. Drop fritters into the oil and fry each fritter until golden brown, about 5 minutes. Fry in batches if required.

5. Remove each fritter from the oil when it is done and transfer to paper towels to drain.

6. To make the sauce, stir all the ingredients together in a medium bowl until thoroughly combined.

7. When all the fritters are fried, sprinkle them with salt. Serve warm, with yoghurt sauce and lemon wedges.

RED CAPSICUM TART ON ALMOND CRUST

INGREDIENTS

Almond meal crust

2 cups (250g, 8oz) almond meal

3 garlic cloves, minced

1 tsp dried thyme

½ tsp salt

¼ tsp pepper

1/3 cup (80ml, 3fl oz) olive oil

1 tbsp plus 1 tsp water

Filling

Olive oil, for frying

2 red onions, finely chopped

3 red capsicum, deseeded and halved

2 tomatoes, finely chopped

150g (5oz) rocket

Parmesan cheese, grated, to garnish

1 tbsp black sesame seeds, to garnish

METHOD

1. Preheat oven to 200°C (400°F, Gas Mark 6) and grease a large tart dish. Preheat the grill to high.

2. In a mixing bowl, stir together the almond meal, garlic, thyme, salt and pepper. Pour in the olive oil and water and stir until the mixture is thoroughly combined.

3. Press dough evenly into tart dish. Place in oven and bake for 20 minutes, until the crust is firm and golden. Remove from oven and set aside. Leave oven on.

4. Meanwhile, place the capsicum under the grill for 6-8 minutes, turning frequently, until the skin is blackened. Transfer to a bowl, cover with plastic wrap and leave to cool for 15 minutes. When cooled, peel off and discard skins and dice the flesh.

5. Heat olive oil in a large frying pan over medium high heat. Add onions and fry for 1-2 minutes. Reduce heat and cook gently for 8-10 minutes until caramelised. Turn up the heat, add the capsicum and tomatoes and cook for 5 minutes. Remove from heat. Add rocket and stir to combine.

6. Spoon the mixture onto the base and place in the oven for 10 minutes to warm through.

7. Garnish with grated Parmesan and black seasame seeds, to serve.

WHITE BEAN, SPINACH AND CORN PIZZA

INGREDIENTS

1 x400g (14oz) can white beans (cannellini, great northern or navy), rinsed and drained

3 cloves garlic, chopped

1 ready-made thin pizza crust

¼ tsp salt

¼ tsp pepper

8-10 cherry tomatoes, halved

Handful of baby spinach leaves

¼ cup (40g, 1½oz) sweetcorn kernals

⅛ red onion, finely sliced

METHOD

1. Preheat oven to 220°C (425°F, Gas Mark 7) and line a baking tray with greaseproof paper.

2. Place half of the beans and garlic in food processor and process until smooth.

3. Spread bean paste over pizza crust.

4. Add remaining beans, salt, pepper, tomatoes, spinach, corn and onion. Place on baking sheet.

5. Place in the oven and bake for 10 minutes. Serve garnished with fresh basil leaves.

SQUASH AND ZUCCHINI FRITTERS WITH MUSHROOMS

INGREDIENTS

350g (12oz) zucchini, grated

350g (12oz) squash, grated

1 tsp salt

¼ cup (30g, 1oz) plain flour

¼ cup (30g, 1oz) Parmesan cheese, grated

1 garlic clove, minced

1 egg, beaten

½ tsp salt

Pinch of pepper

110g (4oz) butter

230g (8oz) oyster mushrooms

2 tbsps olive oil

Flat leaf parsley, to serve

METHOD

1. Place grated zucchini and squash in a large colander over the sink. Sprinkle salt and toss to combine. Leave to sit for 10 minutes, then squeeze out any excess water.

2. Place zucchini, squash, flour, Parmesan, garlic, egg, salt and pepper in a large mixing bowl and stir to combine.

3. Heat the butter in a large frying pan over a medium heat. Add the mushrooms and cook for 5 minutes until tender.

4. Heat olive oil in a large frying pan over medium high heat. Drop a heaped tbsp of batter into the pan for each fritter. Flatten with a spatula and cook for 2 minutes until golden brown. Flip and cook on the other side for a further 2 minutes.

5. Serve with sauteed mushrooms and garnished with flat leaf parsley.

SERVES 2 ★ PREP 40MIN (PLUS CHILLING) ★ COOK TIME 45MIN

MEDITERRANEAN VEGETABLE PIE

INGREDIENTS

Pastry

2 cups (250g, 8oz)
plain flour, sifted

190g (7oz) butter, chilled,
diced

60g (2oz) sour cream

1 tsp salt

Filling

Olive oil, for frying

2 cloves garlic, chopped

1 leek, sliced

2 red capsicums,
cut into wedges

1 small eggplant, diced

1 zucchini, sliced

6 eggs, beaten

1¼ cups (310ml, 10fl oz)
cream

1/3 cup (40g, 1½ oz)
Parmesan cheese, grated

½ bunch dill, finely
chopped

6 grape tomatoes, halved

¼ cup (40g, 1½oz)
sweetcorn kernals

8 green olives, roughly
chopped

METHOD

1. Place the flour, butter, sour cream and salt in a food processor and work until the mixture comes together.

2. Transfer to a lightly floured work surface and gently knead for 1 minute, adding a little flour if needed, until soft and malleable. Wrap in plastic wrap and leave to rest in the fridge for 30 minutes.

3. Preheat oven to 190°C (375°F, Gas Mark 5). Grease a deep pie dish or oven proof dish.

4. Heat olive oil in a large frying pan over medium-high heat. Add garlic and leeks and cook, stirring, for 1 minute. Add red capsicums, eggplant and zucchini and cook for a further 2 minutes, or until slightly softened. Allow mixture to cool slightly.

5. In a medium bowl, mix together the egg, cream, Parmesan cheese, dill and season to taste. Add tomatoes, sweetcorn and olives and stir through.

6. Arrange the vegetables on the pastry base and pour cream mixture over the top.

7. Place in the oven and bake for 40 minutes.

8. Garnish with spring onion, fresh dill, olives and lemon slices.

SERVES 4 ★ PREP 35MIN (PLUS CHILLING) ★ COOK TIME 50MIN

FIG AND GOAT'S CHEESE TART

INGREDIENTS

Pastry

1¼ cups (155g, 5oz) plain flour

½ tsp salt

160g (6oz) chilled butter, cut into pieces

1 to 2 tbsps ice water

Filling

Olive oil, for frying

3 red onions, very thinly sliced

280g (10oz) goat's cheese

1 tsp fresh thyme

½ tsp salt

¼ tsp pepper

6 fresh figs, sliced

Balsamic vinegar and honey, to finish

METHOD

1. Combine flour and salt in a large bowl. Add butter and rub with fingertips until it resembles coarse crumbs. Gradually add water, until the mixture begins to hold together. Gather dough into a ball and flatten into a thick disk. Wrap in plastic wrap and refrigerate for 30 minutes.

2. Pre heat oven to 200°C (400°F, Gas Mark 6) and grease a shallow tart pan.

3. On a lightly floured surface, roll out the dough. Press into the pan and trim the edges, leaving a slight overhang around the rim. Refrigerate for 30 minutes.

4. Prick bottom of pastry shell with fork. Line the pastry with baking paper, and fill with dried beans, then place in the oven and blind bake for 20 minutes. Remove beans and paper and return to oven to bake for a further 5 minutes. Remove from oven and cool completely on wire rack.

5. In the meantime, heat the olive oil in a large frying pan over medium high heat. Add the onions and fry for 5 minutes until soft. Reduce heat to low and continue to cook for 15 minutes, until caramelised.

6. Spread the caramelised onion onto the pastry shell and bake in the oven for 10 minutes until pastry is golden at the edges.

7. Remove from the oven and transfer to a wire rack to cool for 5 to 10 minutes. When cooled, arrange figs and goat's cheese on top.

8. Serve warm or at room temperature, drizzled with balsamic vinegar and honey.

LENTIL BURGER

INGREDIENTS

Oil, for frying

½ onion, finely chopped

1 carrot, grated

2 cloves garlic, minced

1 zucchini, grated

1 x 400g (14oz) can brown lentils

1 tomato, roughly chopped

3 tbsp rice flour

¼ tsp salt

⅛ tsp pepper

1 egg

1 tsp mustard

¾ cup (90g, 3oz) breadcrumbs (or rice crumbs)

Bread rolls, to serve

Butter lettuce, large tomatoes, sliced, and onion rings, to serve

METHOD

1. Heat oil in a large frying pan over medium-low heat. Add the onion and cook for 5 minutes, until softened. Add garlic, zucchini and carrot, and cook, stirring, for 3 minutes until softened. Drain off excess liquid.

2. Place ingredients in the food processor and process until mixture comes together.

3. Form the mixture into 6 patties. Place in the refrigerator to chill for 15 minutes.

4. Heat the oil in a large frying pan over medium heat and cook the burgers, in batches, for 2 minutes each side until golden.

5. Open the bread rolls and line the bottom half with butter lettuce, sliced tomato and onion. Add the patty and then top with bun.

PARMESAN ZUCCHINI CRISPS

INGREDIENTS

2 zucchini, sliced

1 tbsp olive oil

¼ cup (7g, ¾ oz) freshly grated Parmesan

¼ cup (30g, 1oz) breadcrumbs

⅛ tsp salt

⅛ tsp pepper

METHOD

1. Preheat the oven to 230°C (450°F, Gas Mark 8) and grease a baking tray.

2. In a medium bowl, toss the zucchini with the oil.

3. In a small bowl, combine the Parmesan, breadcrumbs, salt and pepper. Dip each round into the Parmesan mixture, coating it evenly on both sides, pressing the coating on to stick.

4. Place coated zucchini in a single layer on the baking sheet.

5. Place in the oven and bake the zucchini rounds for 25 minutes until brown and crispy. Serve immediately.

BLACK BEAN BURGER

INGREDIENTS

½ cup (100g, 3oz) quinoa

1 x 400g (14oz) can black beans, drained and rinsed

½ cup (185g, 6oz) whole wheat breadcrumbs

½ onion, chopped

½ cup (15g, ½ oz) spinach, chopped

¼ cup (40g, 1½ oz) frozen corn kernels

2 garlic cloves, minced

1 tsp chilli powder

½ tsp cumin

1 tbsp tomato paste

Olive oil, for frying

Wholemeal bread rolls and salad filling, to serve

METHOD

1. Bring ⅔ cup (160ml, 5fl oz) salted water to a boil in a saucepan. Add quinoa, cover, and reduce heat to medium. Simmer for 15 minutes, until liquid has absorbed and quinoa is tender. Set aside.

2. Put black beans, quinoa, breadcrumbs, onion, spinach, corn, garlic, chilli powder, cumin and tomato paste into a mixing bowl. Mix everything together well, using hands or a wooden spoon.

3. Heat the oil in a large frying pan over medium heat. Divide black bean mixture into four equal patties. Cook patties for 5 minutes on each side, until browned on the outside. Cook in batches if necessary.

4. Serve on bread rolls with salad.

NOODLES, PASTA AND RICE

LINGUINE ARRABBIATA

INGREDIENTS

400g (14oz) linguine

¼ cup (50ml, 2fl oz) olive oil

3 cloves garlic, crushed

3 fresh red chillies, sliced

2 x 400g (14oz) cans whole tomatoes

¾ cup (200ml, 7fl oz) vegetable stock

½ cup (60g, 2oz) Parmesan cheese, finely grated (retaining some for garnish)

Small handful flat leaf parsley leaves, chopped (retaining some for garnish)

Salt and olive oil, to serve

METHOD

1. In a medium saucepan of boiling salted water, cook linguine until almost cooked. Drain.

2. Meanwhile, heat the oil, garlic, and chillies in a large frying pan over a medium heat. Cook for 5 minutes, until garlic is very lightly golden, but not brown.

3. Add tomatoes, stir to combine, and bring to a bare simmer. Add pasta and stir.

4. Add vegetable stock to the pan and increase heat to bring pasta and sauce to a vigorous simmer.

5. Cook, stirring occasionally, for 1-2 minutes until pasta is al dente.

6. Remove from heat and stir in cheese and parsley.

7. Drizzle with olive oil, season with salt and garnish with fresh parsley and Parmesan cheese.

VEGETARIAN PAELLA

INGREDIENTS

2 tbsps olive oil

1 onion, chopped

1 green capsicum, sliced

1 red capsicum, sliced

1 carrot, julienned

2 garlic cloves, minced

3 cups (465g, 12oz) white rice

1 tsp saffron threads, crushed (or ½ tsp ground saffron)

2 cups (500ml, 1pt) vegetable stock

1 cup (250ml, 8fl oz) water

½ tsp dried thyme

2 tomatoes, finely chopped

150g (5oz) green beans, trimmed

20 black olives

2 tbsps fresh flat leaf parsley, chopped

¼ tsp freshly ground black pepper

Flat leaf parsley, chopped, and lemon wedges, to garnish

METHOD

1. Heat olive oil in a large deep-sided pan or wok over medium-high heat. Add onion, capsicum, carrot, and garlic and saute for 5 minutes.

2. Stir in the rice and saffron threads, then add vegetable stock and water. Bring to a boil. Cover, reduce heat, and simmer for 15 minutes until rice is tender.

3. Stir in tomato, green beans, olives, parsley and black pepper. Cook 3 minutes or until rice is tender and mixture is thoroughly heated.

4. Garnish with chopped fresh parsley and lemon wedges to serve.

ASIAN NOODLES

INGREDIENTS

450g (1lb) soba noodles

2 cloves garlic, sliced

½ red onion, sliced

1 small eggplant,
julienned

1 red capsicum, julienned

1 yellow capsicum,
julienned

3 spring onions, sliced

100g (3½oz) green beans,
trimmed and halved

2 tbsps toasted
sesame oil

3 tbsps tamari
(or soy sauce)

1 tsp cayenne pepper

Small piece ginger,
peeled, to garnish

1 tbsp sesame seeds,
to garnish

METHOD

1. Place a large saucepan of water over a medium high heat and bring to the boil. Add noodles and cook according to package instructions. Drain and set aside.

2. Heat 4-6 tablespoons of water in a wok over high heat. Add garlic, and onion to the wok and stir-fry for 5 minutes, until tender. Add the eggplant and stir-fry for a further 5 minutes until tender, then add the capsicums, spring onions and beans and fry for another 3-4 minutes until just soft. Remove vegetables from wok and set aside.

3. Place the noodles in the hot wok. Add sesame oil, tamari, and cayenne pepper and toss for 5 minutes until the noodles absorb the sauce. Return the vegetables to the wok and toss a few times to combine.

4. To serve, grate fresh ginger over the top, and garnish with spring onions and sesame seeds.

MEDITERRANEAN ROAST VEGETABLE PASTA

INGREDIENTS

1 small eggplant, diced

1 zucchini, diced

1 red onion, thinly sliced

2 garlic cloves, unpeeled

2 tbsp olive oil

Salt and pepper, to season

2 fresh tomatoes, quartered

200g (7oz) penne pasta

Handful fresh dill, leaves picked

½ lemon (optional)

Sesame seeds, to garnish

METHOD

1. Heat oven to 200°C (400°F, Gas Mark 6) and line a large oven dish or baking tray with greaseproof paper.

2. In a large mixing bowl, toss eggplant, zucchini, red onion and garlic together with the olive oil. Season with salt and pepper. Transfer to baking dish or tray. Set bowl aside.

3. Place tray in the oven and roast for 20 minutes. Remove from oven and add the tomatoes, then return to oven to roast for a further 10 minutes.

4. Cook the pasta until al dente. Drain and reserve 4 tbsp of cooking water. Tip pasta, water and roasted vegetables into large mixing bowl and toss to combine.

5. Transfer to a serving dish and squeeze fresh lemon, if using, over the top and sprinkle with sesame seeds.

HOMEMADE PESTO WITH ZUCCHINI NOODLES

INGREDIENTS

Pesto

1 cup (30g, 1oz) basil leaves

¼ cup (30g, 1oz) pine nuts, toasted

¼ cup (60ml, 2fl oz) olive oil

1 clove garlic, crushed

½ tsp salt

¼ tsp pepper

¼ cup (30g, 1oz) Parmesan, grated

4 zucchini

10-15 cherry tomatoes, halved

½ cup (60g, 2oz) Parmesan, finely grated

Handful of basil leaves, to garnish

METHOD

1. Place the basil, pine nuts, olive oil, garlic, salt and pepper into a food processor and pulse until smooth. Add the Parmesan and pulse until a thicker consistency is reached. Cover and place in the refrigerator until ready.

2. Finely julienne the zucchini using a kitchen knife or mandolin. Steam in a steamer for 2 minutes or blanch in a pan of boiling water for 30 seconds.

3. Place pasta, tomatoes and pesto in a large bowl and toss well to thoroughly coat the pasta.

4. Garnish with Parmesan cheese and basil leaves to serve.

SERVES 4 ★ PREP 40MIN (PLUS RESTING) ★ COOK TIME 50MIN

HOMEMADE BEETROOT TAGLIATELLE AND PESTO

INGREDIENTS

Beetroot tagliatelle

2 small beetroot

2 eggs

1 egg yolk

1 tbsp olive oil

1 tsp salt

2 cups (250g, 8oz) plain flour

Beetroot pesto

1 large beetroot

3 tbsps pine nuts

3 tbsps olive oil

3 tbsps Parmesan, grated

2 garlic cloves, crushed

Salt and pepper, to taste

Black poppy seeds, steamed rocket and Parmesan, to serve

METHOD

1. Preheat the oven to 230°C (450°F, Gas Mark 8).

2. Wrap all the beetroot (for pasta and pesto) in foil and place in the oven for 45 minutes or until soft. Remove from oven and separate out the 2 small beetroot needed for pasta and 1 large beetroot needed for the pesto. Set both sets aside to cool. When cool, slip off the skins and dice roughly.

3. Place the beetroots for the pasta in a blender with the eggs, egg yolk, oil and salt, and pulse until smooth.

4. Sift the flour over a large bowl. Add the beetroot puree and mix until fully incorporated and a dough forms.

5. Knead dough by hand for about 10 minutes or until it turns smooth and elastic. Place in a bowl, cover with plastic wrap and allow to rest for 1 hour.

6. Roll out the dough according to your pasta machine's instructions, or roll by hand with a rolling pin. Brush sheet lightly with flour, roll up, and, using a sharp knife, cut into strips, then unroll.

7. Heat a frying pan over high heat. Add pine nuts and dry fry, stirring, for 2-3 minutes, until golden and fragrant.

8. Combine all pesto ingredients in a blender and pulse until a smooth paste forms.

9. Bring a large pan of salted water to the boil. Drop in pasta and cook for 2 minutes.

10. Arrange pasta in bowls with pesto on top. Sprinkle with poppy seeds and serve with steamed rocket and Parmesan.

BEAN PILAF WITH YOGHURT

INGREDIENTS

2 tbsps butter

1 red onion, halved and thinly sliced

185g (6oz) basmati rice

2 cups (500ml, 1pt) vegetable stock

150g (5oz) green beans

200g (7oz) edamame beans

½ cup (20g, ¾ oz) dill, leaves picked (reserve some for garnish)

100g (3½oz) fresh spinach

100g (3½oz) Greek yoghurt

1 tbsp milk

½ garlic clove, crushed

Black pepper, to serve

METHOD

1. Heat the butter in a medium-sized saucepan over a medium-high heat. Add the onions and fry for 5 minutes, until soft. Add the rice and stir for 1 minute.

2. Pour in the stock bring to the boil. Cover, reduce heat and simmer for 7 minutes.

3. Add the beans, edamame and dill and cook for a further 5 minutes until the liquid has been absorbed into the rice. Add the spinach and stir to to combine. Replace lid.

4. Meanwhile, stir the yoghurt, milk and garlic together in a small bowl. Spoon yoghurt on top of the rice, then sprinkle with remaining dill and black pepper to serve.

TOFU STIRFRY

INGREDIENTS

3 cups (465g, 12oz) brown rice

2 tbsps olive oil

3 cloves garlic, minced

1 medium piece ginger, finely chopped

225g (8oz, ½lb) baked, flavored tofu, cubed

3 carrots, finely julienned

8 asparagus spears, halved

3 tbsps soy sauce

1 tsp toasted sesame oil

3 spring onions, sliced

METHOD

1. Bring a large pan of salted water to the boil and cook the rice according the instructions on the packet. Drain and set aside, covered, to keep warm.

2. Heat the olive oil in a large frying pan over medium-high heat. Add the garlic and ginger and fry for 1 minutes until aromatic.

3. Add the tofu and fry for 4-5 minutes, until golden brown, turning occasionally to ensure even cooking.Add carrots and asparagus and cook, stirring, for 4 minutes or until just tender. Add soy sauce and sesame oil and lightly toss to combine.

4. Serve tofu on top of rice and garnished with spring onion.

TEMPEH AND TOFU NOODLE BOWL

INGREDIENTS

Sauce

4 tbsps soy sauce

1 tbsp sesame oil

1 tbsp rice wine vinegar

1 tsp ginger, grated

2 cloves garlic, minced

1 tbsp brown sugar

Pinch of crushed
red pepper

Bowl

225g (8oz, ½ lb) tempeh,
thinly sliced

180g (6oz) udon noodles

1 tbsp vegetable oil

1 carrot, julienned

1 red capsicum,
julienned

1 bunch baby bok choy,
roughly chopped

2 spring onions,
sliced

6 deep fried tofu puffs

METHOD

1. Place the sauce ingredients in a bowl and whisk to combine. Add the tempeh and rotate to coat. Cover and place in the fridge to marinate for 10-15 minutes. Remove with a slotted spoon, retaining marinade. Pat tempeh dry.

2. Place a medium saucepan of salted water on a high heat and bring to the boil. Cook noodles according to the instructions on the packet.

3. Heat oil in a large frying pan over high heat. Add tempeh and cook for 5 minutes, until golden brown. Set aside.

4. Add carrot, capsicum, bok choy and spring onions and half of the tempeh marinade and cook for 3-4 minutes. Add noodles and remaining marinade and cook for a further 2 minutes, coating the noodles.

5. Serve in bowls with tempeh and tofu puffs on top.

SPAGHETTI AL POMODORO

INGREDIENTS

2 tbsp olive oil

15-20 cherry or mini roma tomatoes, halved

1 red capsicum, seeded and diced

100g (3½ oz) passata

2 garlic cloves, finely sliced

Pinch of chilli flakes (optional)

1 tbsp capers

10 black olives, unpitted

1 tsp sugar

½ tsp salt

¼ tsp pepper

375g (13oz) spaghetti

½ cup (20g, ¾oz) parsley leaves, chopped

2 tbsp Parmesan cheese, finely grated

METHOD

1. Combine the fresh tomatoes, capsicum, passata, garlic, chilli flakes, if using, capers, olives, olive oil, sugar, salt and pepper in a large saucepan set over a medium-high heat. Cook, stirring for 1-2 minutes, then leave to simmer for 20 minutes until thick.

2. Bring a large saucepan of salted water to the boil. Add pasta and cook until al dente. Drain, reserving a few tablespoons of cooking water.

3. Add pasta and reserved water to the sauce in the pan, and toss well for a minute or two over a low heat until the pasta has absorbed most of the sauce.

4. Serve hot, scattered with parsley leaves and Parmesan cheese.

SZECHUAN COLD NOODLES

INGREDIENTS

200g (7oz) egg noodles

2 tsps sesame oil

1 cucumber, julienned

Sauce

3 tsp sugar

1 tsp rice vinegar

½ tbsp tahini

Pinch of salt

1 tbsp tamari (or soy sauce)

1 tbsp chilli oil

3 garlic cloves, minced

Small piece ginger, minced

To serve

1-2 red chilli, chopped finely

1 tbsp white sesame seeds

Sprig of mint

METHOD

1. Bring a pan of water to the boil and cook the noodles according to the directions on the packet. Drain, reserving a small amount of cooking water.

2. Return noodles to the pot. Add oil and stir well to avoid sticking. Set aside to cool.

3. Combine all the sauce ingredients with a tablespoon of the reserved water and stir well.

4. When noodles have cooled, add cucumber and sauce to the pot. Mix well to combine

5. Serve cold, garnished with red chilli, sesame seeds and mint.

PUMPKIN RISOTTO

INGREDIENTS

1 small butternut
pumpkin, cubed

Olive oil, for frying

1½ cups (375ml, 13fl oz)
vegetable stock

55g (2oz) butter

2 medium (300g, 10oz)
onions, chopped

2 cloves garlic, finely
chopped

2 cups (310g, 8oz) arborio
rice

½ cup (125ml, 4fl oz) dry
white wine

60g (2oz) mascarpone

½ cup (60g, 2oz)
Parmesan cheese, grated,
2 tbsps reserved for
garnishing

METHOD

1. Preheat the oven to 200°C (400°F, Gas Mark 6) and line a
    baking tray with greaseproof paper.

2. Toss the pumpkin in olive oil and season with salt. Scatter in one
    layer in the baking tray and place in the oven. Roast for 25 minutes
    or until tender and golden. Reserve ¼ of the pumpkin. Cover to keep
    warm.

3. Meanwhile, bring stock to a gentle simmer in a medium saucepan.
    Reduce heat to very low and cover pan.

4. Melt butter in a large saucepan over a medium high heat. Add onion
    and cook, stirring, for 3-4 minutes until soft. Add garlic and rice and
    cook, stirring to coat well, for 1 minute. Pour in wine and simmer,
    uncovered, until liquid has reduced.

5. Reduce heat to low and add stock to the rice ½ cup at a time until
    the liquid has fully absorbed. Stir constantly. Stir in pumpkin half
    way through the process. The risotto is done
    when the rice is tender but still firm to bite and risotto is creamy.
    Add more stock, if required to achieve this consistency and cook for
    a further 5 minutes.

6. Remove risotto from heat. Stir in the mascarpone and Parmesan
    cheese. Season. Serve topped with reserved Parmesan cheese.

STUFFED RICOTTA SHELLS

INGREDIENTS

15-20 jumbo pasta shells

2 tbsps olive oil

2 tsps fresh garlic, minced

1 bunch fresh spinach, leaves picked and chopped

340g (12oz) ricotta cheese

1 cup (125g, 4oz) mozarella cheese, grated

½ cup (60,g, 2oz) Parmesan cheese, finely grated

1 egg

1 tbsp fresh basil, chopped

1 tsp salt

½ tsp pepper

1 cup (250ml, 8fl oz) marinara sauce (bottled)

Parmesan and fresh pepper, to serve

METHOD

1. Preheat the oven to 190°C (375°F, Gas Mark 5).

2. Bring a large saucepan of salted water to the boil. Add pasta and cook until almost al dente. Drain and set aside.

3. Meanwhile, heat the olive oil in a large frying pan over a medium-high heat. Add the garlic and cook for 1-2 minutes, until golden. Add the spinach and cook for a further 1-2 minutes, stirring occasionally, until the leaves begin to wilt but are still bright green. Set aside to cool.

4. In a large bowl, mix the spinach, ricotta, mozzarella, Parmesan, egg, basil and salt and pepper until thoroughly combined.

5. Pour half of the marinara sauce into the bottom of baking dish.

6. Stuff each pasta shell with the spinach and ricotta mixture, and place in the baking dish.

7. Cover with the remaining sauce and bake covered for 25 minutes.

8. Serve warm with a dusting of Parmesan and plenty of fresh ground pepper.

BAKED BROCCOLI CHEESE

INGREDIENTS

1 head of broccoli, cut into florets

550g (1¼lb) farfalle pasta

1 tbsp butter

½ cup (60g, 2oz) plain flour

½ cup (125ml, 4fl oz) milk

½ tsp salt

¼ tsp pepper

1 cup (125g, 4oz) mozarella cheese, grated

½ cup (100g, 3½ oz) sour cream

1 cup (125g, 4oz) Parmesan cheese, finely grated

METHOD

1. Preheat the oven to 180°C (350°F, Gas Mark 4) and grease an ovenproof baking dish.

2. Cook broccoli in a large saucepan of boiling water for 3-5 minutes, until tender. Drain and set aside.

3. Bring a large saucepan of salted water to the boil. Add pasta and cook until almost al dente. Drain and set aside.

4. Melt butter over medium heat in a small saucepan. Add flour and whisk until well combined, then add milk, salt, pepper and mozarella cheese. Reduce heat to a low simmer and continue to whisk until sauce has thickened slightly. Stir in sour cream.

5. Place broccoli and pasta in a baking dish and then pour cream sauce over the top. Top with Parmesan.

6. Place in the oven and bake uncovered for 35 minutes.

PENNE WITH SPINACH SAGE PESTO

INGREDIENTS

½ cup (60g, 2oz) walnuts

2 cups (60g, 2oz) fresh spinach, plus leaves for garnish finely chopped

½ cup (20g, ¾o z) fresh sage leaves

¾ cup (90g, 3oz) pecorino or Parmesan cheese, grated

Salt and pepper, to taste

⅓ cup (80ml, 3fl oz) extra-virgin olive oil

455g (1lb) penne pasta

1 small head broccoli, broken into florets

1 cup (170g, 6oz) peas (fresh or frozen)

Parmesan or pecorino, grated, chopped walnuts and sage leaves, to serve

METHOD

1. Warm a frying pan and dry-roast walnuts until golden. Remove from heat and place on paper towels.

2. Blanch spinach in warm water, and quickly transfer to an ice bath. Drain and thoroughly pat dry spinach leaves.

3. Place dried spinach, sage leaves and walnuts in a food processer with cheese and salt and pepper to taste.

4. Add oil gradually, until pesto forms a smooth paste.

5. Bring a large saucepan of salted water to the boil. Add pasta and cook until almost al dente. Drain and set aside.

6. Bring another saucepan of water to the boil. Add broccoli and cook for 5 minutes until tender, but still crunchy. After 2 minutes, add peas. Drain.

7. In a large bowl, mix pesto through penne, until just coated. Add vegetables and toss to combine.

8. Serve with additional grated cheese, spinach leaves and fresh sage.

EGG FRIED RICE

INGREDIENTS

2 cups (310g, 8oz)
white rice

4 cups (1L, 2pt) water

1 carrot, finely diced

½ cup (80g, 3oz) green
peas (fresh or frozen)

2 tbsps vegetable oil

2 eggs

2 tbsps tamari
(or soy sauce)

1 tbsp sesame oil

2 spring onions, chopped,
to garnish

METHOD

1. Combine rice and water in a saucepan over a medium heat and bring to a boil. Reduce heat, cover, and simmer for 15 minutes.

2. In a small saucepan, boil carrots in water about 3 minutes. Drop peas into boiling water, and cook for 2 minutes more, then drain.

3. Heat a wok over a high heat. Pour in oil, and then add carrots and peas. Stir-fry for 30 seconds, then crack in eggs, stirring quickly to scramble with vegetables.

4. Stir in cooked rice. Pour in the tamari, and toss rice to coat. Drizzle with sesame oil, and toss again.

5. Serve garnished with spring onions.

RAW PAD THAI

INGREDIENTS

Peanut sauce

¼ cup (90g, 3oz) peanut butter

1 clove of garlic, minced

2 tbsps tamari (or soy sauce)

1 tbsp toasted sesame oil

Small piece ginger, minced

1 lime, juiced

Noodles

¼ small head of white cabbage, shredded

2 green zucchini, julienned

2 yellow zucchini, julienned

1 cucumber, julienned

½ red onion, finely sliced

4-5 small cauliflower florets, parboiled

½ red capsicum, sliced

Toppings

Pinch of chilli powder

1 tbsp hemp seeds

METHOD

1. Place the ingredients for the peanut sauce in a food processor, and pulse until smooth. Adjust seasoning to taste. Slowly add 3-4 tbsps of water, to achieve the desired consistency.

2. In a large bowl, toss cabbage, zucchini, cucumber, onion, cauliflower and capsicum together until combined. Gradually add the peanut sauce and keep tossing until the noodles are well and evenly coated.

3. To serve, garnish with chilli powder and hemp seeds.

SERVES 6 ★ PREP 1HR (PLUS RESTING) ★ COOK TIME 50MIN

HOMEMADE RAVIOLI

INGREDIENTS

Sauce

⅓ cup (80ml, 3fl oz) olive oil

2 onions, finely chopped

4 garlic cloves, minced

4 cups (1L, 2pt) passata

1 bunch basil, leaves chopped (retain a few for garnish)

Pasta dough

1 tsp olive oil

1 tsp salt

¼ cup (60ml, 2fl oz) warm water

4 cups (500g, 1lb) plain flour

200g (7oz) fine semolina

6 eggs

Filling

1 tbsp olive oil

2 bunches spinach, leaves picked, steamed and chopped

800g (1¾ lb) firm ricotta

1½ cup (190g, 6oz) grated Parmesan cheese

2 egg yolks

½ tsp ground nutmeg

METHOD

1. Heat the olive oil in a large saucepan over low heat. Add the onion and garlic and stir for 5 minutes or until soft. Add passata and basil and simmer, partially covered for 40 minutes, until a thick sauce forms.

2. Mix the olive oil, salt and warm water in a small bowl. Sift flour and semolina onto a clean work surface and create a well in the middle. Crack the eggs into the centre of the well, then add oil mixture. Gradually mix the wet ingredients with the flour using fingers until a dough comes together. Knead the dough for 10-15 minutes or until smooth. Shape into a ball, cover in plastic wrap and set aside to rest for 30 minutes.

3. Place filling ingredients in a bowl and stir to combine well. Cover and refrigerate until ready to use.

4. Divide the pasta dough into 4 portions. One piece at a time, flatten the dough on a lightly floured work surface. Pass the pasta several times through the widest setting on a pasta machine, folding it in half each time. Once smooth, reduce the settings one notch at time until the second last setting.

5. Lay the pasta on a floured surface. Place one teaspoon of filling in intervals along the bottom half of the pasta. Fold the top half over, then press the sides to seal well. Place on a tray dusted with semolina, cover and refrigerate until ready to cook.

6. Bring a large saucepan of salted water to the boil. Drop in the ravioli and simmer for 5 minutes or until al dente. Drain. Transfer the ravioli to a large serving dish, spoon over the hot passata, then scatter with basil leaves and black pepper and serve immediately.

RISOTTO WITH PEAR AND GORGONZOLA

INGREDIENTS

4 cups (1L, 2pt) vegetable stock

1 cup (250ml, 8fl oz) dry white wine

1½ tbsps olive oil

1 cup (155g, 4oz) arborio rice

100g (3½ oz) Gorgonzola cheese, crumbled

1 ripe unpeeled pear, cored and diced

Paremesan cheese, grated, for serving

METHOD

1. Bring vegetable stock and white wine to a gentle boil a in saucepan over medium heat. Cover and reduce heat to very low.

2. Heat oil in medium saucepan over medium heat. Add rice and saute for 2 minutes, until translucent.

3. Add 3 cups of stock mixture to rice. Simmer uncovered for 15-20 minutes, stirring often. The risotto is done when the rice is tender but still firm to bite and risotto is creamy. Add more stock, if required to achieve this consistency and cook for a further 5 minutes.

4. Gently stir Gorgonzola and pear through the risotto and cook for 1 minute until cheese starts to melts and pear is heated through.

5. Serve garnished with grated Parmesan.

GOAT'S CHEESE, LEEK AND ASPARAGUS PASTA

INGREDIENTS

225g (8oz, ½ lb) penne pasta

1 bunch asparagus, trimmed and sliced

1½ tbsps butter

1 leek, quartered and thinly sliced

1½ tbsps plain flour

¾ cup (185ml, 6fl oz) milk

½ tbsp lemon zest

⅛ tsp nutmeg

Salt and pepper, to taste

125g (4oz) soft goat's cheese

¼ cup (30g, 1oz) Parmesan, freshly grated

Fresh lemon juice, to serve

METHOD

1. Cook the pasta according to the instructions on the packet. When cooked, remove with a slotted spoon and place in a large bowl. Return water to the boil, then add asparagus. Cook for 2-3 minutes, until just tender. Drain and immediately add to the pasta.

2. Meanwhile, melt the butter in a small saucepan over medium high heat. Add leek and saute for 5 minutes, until soft. Whisk in the flour until dissolved, about 1 minute. Add the milk, lemon zest, nutmeg, salt and pepper. Reduce heat slightly and allow to simmer, whisking occasionally for 4 minutes, until thickened. Add cheeses, stirring until melted and the sauce is smooth.

3. Pour sauce over the pasta and asparagus and toss until evenly coated. Add a squeeze of fresh lemon juice to serve.

SERVES 2 ★ PREP 40MIN ★ COOK TIME 1HR 10MIN

PUMPKIN GNOCCHI

INGREDIENTS

1 large pumpkin,
cut into chunks

½ tsp salt

¼ tsp ground nutmeg

Salt and pepper, to taste

2½ cups (310g, 10oz)
plain flour, plus extra
for dusting

60g (2oz) butter

2 tbsps thyme leaves

Shaved Parmesan and
thyme sprigs, to serve

METHOD

1. Preheat oven to 200°C (400°F, Gas Mark 6) and line a baking tray with greaseproof paper.

2. Scatter pumpkin in a single layer on tray. Sprinkle salt over the top. Place in the oven and cook for 1 hour or until tender. Set aside to cool slightly.

3. Place pumpkin in a large bowl and and mash until smooth. Add nutmeg. Taste and season with salt and pepper.

4. Add flour to the pumpkin mash and mix into a sticky dough that holds together.

5. Divide the dough into 4 even portions. Roll 1 portion out on a lightly floured surface into a sausage. Cut the dough into the desired size for gnocchi. With floured hands, roll each piece of dough into a ball. Place gnocchi on lined tray. Repeat with remaining dough.

6. Bring a large saucepan of salted water to the boil over a medium high heat. Cook gnocci in batches according to size of pan. Cook each batch, uncovered, for 2-3 minutes. Remove with a slotted spoon and drain before transferring to a plate. Cover with foil to keep warm until all gnocchi is cooked.

7. Heat a large frying pan over a medium-high heat and melt butter. Add thyme leaves and cook for 1-2 minutes until aromatic. Add the gnocchi and pan fry for 2-3 minutes, stirring carefully, until golden brown.

8. Divide the gnocchi among serving plates and garnish with Parmesan and sprigs of thyme.

MISO SOBA NOODLE SOUP

INGREDIENTS

2 tsps sesame oil

2 tsps fresh garlic, minced

Small piece ginger, minced

1 tbsp soy sauce

4 cups (1L, 2pt) vegetable stock

125g (4oz) soba (buckwheat) noodles

6-8 button mushrooms, sliced

1 sheet nori, cut into slices

200g (7oz) firm tofu, cubed

2 tbsps miso paste

1 tsp ponzu (optional)

Handful of mixed lettuce leaves

1 spring onion, sliced

2 tsps toasted sesame seeds, to garnish

METHOD

1. Heat the oil in a large saucepan over medium heat. Add the garlic and ginger, and cook, stirring, for 5 minutes until softened. Add the soy sauce, and stir to combine. Cook for a further 1 minute.

2. Add the stock, cover and bring to a boil. Remove the lid, Reduce heat to a gentle simmer and cook uncovered for a further 10 minutes.

3. Add the soba noodles to the ginger broth and cook for 7-8 minutes. After 5 minutes, add the mushrooms and nori to the broth. Cook for 3-5 minutes, until mushrooms are tender. Add tofu and allow to heat through for 1-2 minutes.

4. Add the miso paste and ponzu, if using, to the stock and stir for 30 seconds until combined.

5. Divide the soup between two large bowls. Garnish with spring onions and lettuce leaves.

EGGPLANT PASTA

INGREDIENTS

1-2 eggplants,
cut into cubes

2 tsp salt

Olive oil, for frying

1 onion, finely chopped

4 garlic cloves, finely
chopped

2 tsps chilli flakes

2 tbsps capers

5 large fresh tomatoes,
chopped (or use 1 x 400g
(14oz) can of tomatoes)

2 tbsps tomato puree

2 tbsps fresh basil leaves

salt & freshly ground
black pepper

450g (1lb) spaghetti,
cooked until al dente

Cracked pepper, to
garnish

METHOD

1. Place eggplant in a colander set over the sink and sprinkle with salt. Leave to drain for 20 minutes, then pat dry with kitchen paper.

2. Heat oil for in a frying pan over a medium-high heat. Add eggplant and fry, stirring, for 5 minutes, until golden brown. Remove with a slotted spoon and drain on paper towels.

3. Add onion to the same pan and cook, stirring, for 5 minutes until soft. Then add garlic and chilli flakes or and cook for 1 minute or until garlic just begins to turn colour.

4. Mix in capers, tomatoes, tomato puree and fresh basil. Season with salt and pepper. Cover pan and cook sauce on a low heat for 30 minutes.

5. Add eggplant, stir, and remove from heat.

6. Bring a large saucepan of salted water to the boil. Add pasta and cook until al dente. Drain and return to the pot.

7. Add a cup of sauce to the spaghetti and coat to cover the strands. Then serve the rest of the sauce on the side, and garnish with fresh cracked pepper.

SERVES 4 ★ PREP 30MIN ★ COOK TIME 60MIN

PUMPKIN RICOTTA LASAGNE

INGREDIENTS

1 pumpkin, peeled and diced

2 tsps rosemary, finely chopped

Oil, for brushing

500g (1lb 2oz) ricotta cheese

2 tsps chopped chives

1 egg

½ cup (125ml, 4fl oz) milk

300g (10½ oz) baby spinach leaves

1 pkt lasagne sheets

1 cup (125g, 4oz) cheddar cheese, grated

Handful of pine nuts

METHOD

1. Preheat oven to 180°C (350°F, Gas Mark 4). Line a large baking tray with baking paper and grease a lasagne dish with oil.

2. Place pumpkin pieces in a single layer on baking tray. Brush with oil and sprinkle with rosemary.

3. Roast pumpkin for 25 minutes, or until soft and golden, then mash and set aside. Leave oven on.

4. In a bowl, combine ricotta, chives, egg and milk and mix until creamy.

5. Spoon one-third of the pumpkin mash over base of lasagne dish, followed by half the spinach leaves. Place 1 lasagne sheet on top. Repeat with another layer of pumpkin and spinach then one-third of the ricotta. Repeat with another lasagne sheet, pumpkin and ricotta. Top with last lasagne sheet, spread evenly with remaining ricotta on top. Sprinkle liberally with grated cheese, and pine nuts.

6. Place in the oven and bake for 30 minutes, until golden.

7. Stand for 5 minutes before serving.

DINNER
AND
SIDES

QUINOA AND CORN BURRITOS

INGREDIENTS

1¾ cups (440ml, 15fl oz) water

1 cup (190g, 7oz), rinsed and drained quinoa

1 tbsp olive oil

½ onion, chopped

1 spring onion, sliced

3 ears sweet corn, kernels removed

Salt and pepper, to season

1 x 400g (14oz) can black beans, drained and rinsed

½ cup (100g, 3½ oz) vegetable stock

1 tsp chilli powder

½ tsp smoked paprika

¼ tsp cayenne pepper

1 tomato, finely chopped

3 tbsps fresh coriander, chopped

½ lime, juiced

6 soft tortillas

METHOD

1. Bring salted water to a boil in a saucepan. Add quinoa, cover, and reduce heat to medium. Simmer for 15 minutes, until liquid is absorbed and quinoa is tender. Set aside.

2. Meanwhile, heat oil in a large frying pan over medium-high heat. Add onion, spring onion and corn kernels, season with salt and pepper, then saute for 5 minutes until onion is tender.

3. Add black beans, vegetable stock, chilli powder, smoked paprika, and cayenne pepper then simmer until liquid is nearly absorbed, 4 minutes. Add tomatoes then simmer until tender, 2 minutes. Remove from heat then stir in coriander and lime juice. Set aside.

4. Preheat oven to 180°C (350°F, Gas Mark 4).

5. Heat tortillas according to package instructions.

6. Place open tortilla on a flat surface and place filling along one side. Roll once then tuck in sides and continue rolling to form a burrito. Wrap in foil then place in the oven to bake for 10 minutes.

TEMPEH SATAY KEBABS

INGREDIENTS

1 cup (250ml, 8fl oz) tamari (or soy sauce)

4 cups (1L, 2pt) water

Small piece of ginger, sliced

3 cloves garlic, crushed

1 bay leaf

225g (8oz, ½ lb) tempeh, cut into cubes

²/₃ cup (80g, 3oz) plain flour (or rice flour)

²/₃ cup (80g, 3oz) nutritional yeast

1 tsp salt

Pinch of pepper

Peanut oil, for frying

METHOD

1. Place the tamari, water, ginger, garlic and bay leaf into saucepan over a medium heat. Bring the liquid to a gentle simmer. Add the tempeh and cook, uncovered, for 20 minutes. Drain and set aside to cool.

2. Scatter the flour, nutritional yeast, salt and pepper on a plate or in a shallow dish.

3. Gently roll each tempeh cube through the seasoned flour to coat evenly.

4. Thread tempeh cubes onto a medium bamboo skewers.

5. Heat oil in a large frying pan set over a medium-high heat. Sear on each side for 3 minutes or until golden brown and beginning to char slightly.

6. Serve immediately with sweet chilli sauce.

KALE STIR-FRY

INGREDIENTS

Vegetable oil, for frying

2 cloves garlic, thinly sliced

1 bunch kale, chopped (large stems removed)

Small piece ginger, sliced

2-3 mixed chillis (orange and red), sliced

2 fresh tomatoes, quartered

1 tbsp toasted sesame oil

Pinch of salt

1 tbsp lemon juice

METHOD

1. Heat the oil in a large frying pan or wok over a medium-high heat.

2. Add the garlic, and stir-fry for 30 seconds until aromatic.
   Add ginger and chillis and stir-fry for 2 minutes until aromatic.

3. Add the kale and cook for 2 minutes, until soft but bright green.

4. Add tomatoes, sesame oil, salt and lemon juice and stir-fry for 1 minute, until heated through.

5. Serve immediately.

FALAFEL WITH CREAMY DILL DRESSING

SERVES 4 ★ PREP 35MIN ★ COOK TIME 20MIN

INGREDIENTS

1 x 400g (14oz) can chickpeas, drained

1 onion, chopped

½ bunch parsley leaves

2 cloves garlic, chopped

1 egg, beaten

2 tsp ground cumin

1 tsp ground coriander

1 tsp salt

1 tsp baking powder

1 tbsp black sesame seeds

1 tsp lemon juice

1 tbsp olive oil

1 cup (125g, 4oz) breadcrumbs

Creamy dill dressing

¼ cup (60ml, 2fl oz) sour cream

¼ cup (60ml, 2fl oz) plain Greek yoghurt

1 tbsp olive oil

½ tsp white wine vinegar

2 tbsps dill, finely chopped

METHOD

1. Preheat the oven to 180°C (350°F, Gas Mark 4) and prepare a lined baking tray.

2. Place the chickpeas in a large bowl and mash them until thick and creamy

3. Place onion, parsley and garlic in a blender or food processor and pulse until smooth. Stir into mashed chickpeas.

4. In a small bowl, whisk together egg, cumin, coriander, salt, baking powder, black sesame seeds, lemon juice and olive oil. Stir into chickpea mixture. Gradually add breadcrumbs until mixture holds together. You may not to add all the breadcrumbs.

5. Form mixture into 8 balls, then flatten into patties. Place patties on prepared tray.

6. Place in the oven and bake for 20 minutes, turning once.

7. Meanwhile, to make the dressing, whisk together the sour cream, yoghurt, oil, white wine vinegar and dill until well blended and creamy.

8. Serve felafal balls with creamy dill dressing on top.

CUCUMBER NOODLES WITH ASPARAGUS

INGREDIENTS

2 spring onions,
thinly sliced

Small piece ginger,
finely grated

1 tsp toasted sesame oil

¼ cup (30ml, 1fl oz)
olive oil

1½ tbsps tamari
(or soy sauce)

⅛ tsp red pepper flakes
(optional)

Pinch of salt, to taste

1 bunch mini asparagus,
trimmed and halved

2 large cucumbers,
peeled

Cucumber slices, small
piece of ginger, finely
sliced, fresh mint and
lime wedges, to garnish

METHOD

1. In a large bowl whisk together the spring onions, ginger, toasted sesame oil, olive oil, tamari and red pepper flakes, if using. Season to taste with salt. Set aside.

2. Place a large saucepan of salted water over a medium high heat and bring to the boil. Add asparagus and blanch for 2 minutes. Remove and immediately run asparagus under very cold water.

3. Use a spiralizer or julienne peeler to create long noodles from the peeled cucumbers. Place in a large bowl.

4. Pour sauce over the noodles and toss to coat well.

5. Serve the noodles in bowls, garnished with extra cucumber slices, fresh ginger slices, mint and lime wedges.

SERVES 6 ★ PREP 20MIN ★ COOK TIME 40MIN

ZUCCHINI THREE-CHEESE CASSEROLE

INGREDIENTS

6 medium zucchini, thinly sliced

2 tbsps butter

½ onion, finely chopped

1 garlic clove, minced

2 tsps fresh (or 1 tsp dried) oregano

1 x 220g (8oz) can tomato sauce

1 cup (125g, 4oz) mozzarella cheese, grated

½ cup (60g, 2oz) cheddar cheese, grated

1 cup (125g, 4oz) Parmesan cheese, grated

Chives and spring onion, chopped, to garnish

METHOD

1. Preheat oven to 200°C (400°F, Gas Mark 6) and grease a casserole dish.

2. Place zucchini in colander and sprinkle with salt. Let stand 10 minutes, then squeeze out moisture.

3. Melt butter in a large frying pan over medium heat. Fry onion for 3 minutes until soft. Add zucchini slices, garlic and oregano and fry for 2 minutes.

4. Layer the bottom of the casserole with half of the zucchini onion mixture, then add half the tomato sauce and half of the mozarella cheese. Repeat with the other half of the zucchini, tomato, mozarella and cheddar cheese.

5. Place in the oven and bake uncovered for 20 minutes.

6. Remove from the oven and add Parmesan cheese. Return to the oven and cook for a further 15 minutes until cheese is nicely browned.

7. Serve garnished with chive and spring onion.

SERVES 2 ★ PREP 20MIN ★ COOK TIME 35MIN

BUCKWHEAT MINI CASSEROLE

INGREDIENTS

½ cup (100g, 3oz)
buckwheat groats

2 tbsps amaranth flour
(or plain flour)

1 tbsp chia seeds

Olive oil, for frying

1 onion, chopped

250g (9oz) baby spinach
leaves

Salt and pepper, to taste

1 cup (125g, 4oz)
cottage cheese

75g (3oz) cheddar cheese

½ tsp nutmeg

¼ cup (30g, 1oz) toasted
walnuts, chopped

2 eggs

METHOD

1. Preheat oven to 190°C (375°F, Gas Mark 5).

2. Bring 2 cups (500ml, 1pt) salted water and to a boil in a medium saucepan. Add buckwheat groats, amaranth and chia. Cover, reduce heat and simmer for 15 minutes, stirring occasionally, until mixture is creamy and water is absorbed.

3. Heat the oil in a medium frying pan over a medium high heat and fry onion for 5 minutes, until translucent. Reduce heat to low and add spinach. Season with salt and pepper. Stir for 1 minute, until spinach is wilted. Remove from heat and set aside.

4. In a mixing bowl, combine cottage cheese, cheddar cheese and nutmeg. Fold into spinach mixture and add toasted walnuts. Mix until well combined.

5. Divide buckwheat mixture between 2 individual-sized ovenproof dishes and spread evenly. Make a small well in the centre of each. Crack the eggs into the well.

6. Place in the oven and bake for 15 minutes, until the egg has set and golden crust formed.

MISO GLAZED EGGPLANT

INGREDIENTS

Oil, for brushing

1 medium eggplant

¼ cup (60ml, 2fl oz) dashi

1 tbsp mirin

1 tbsp sake

2 tsps sugar

1 tbsp miso

Sesame seeds, to garnish

METHOD

1. Preheat the oven to 180°C (350°F, Gas Mark 4).

2. Slice eggplant in half, then make deep cuts in the surface in a criss cross pattern. Brush with oil.

3. Place in the oven and bake for 30 to 45 minutes until the eggplant is tender.

4. Meanwhile bring dashi, mirin, sake and sugar to a gentle boil in a saucepan over a medium heat. Add miso and stir to combine. Remove from heat.

5. Preheat grill to a medium setting.

6. Remove eggplant from oven, and pour over the sauce. Sprinkle with sesame seeds.

7. Place eggplant under the grill for 3-4 minutes until caramelised.

SERVES 6 ★ PREP 10MIN ★ COOK TIME 10MIN

KALE CHIPS

INGREDIENTS

1 bunch kale, washed
and dried

1 tbsp olive oil

1 tsp salt

METHOD

1. Preheat oven to 175°C (350°F, Gas Mark 4). Line a baking tray.

2. Remove stems from kale. Cut or tear leaves into bite-sized pieces.
    Place on baking tray and drizzle with olive oil. Season with salt.

3. Bake for 10 minutes, until edges of kale are lightly golden, but not
    burnt.

GREEN VEGETABLE BIBIMBAP

INGREDIENTS

Bibimbap sauce

2 tbsps tamari (or soy sauce)

2 tsps spicy Korean chilli seasoning

2 tsps honey

1 tbsps toasted sesame oil

1 tsps rice vinegar (or lemon juice)

Rice

1 cup (155g, 4oz) sushi rice (or multi grain rice)

Toppings

6-8 cucumber slices

2 eggs

4-6 small broccoli florets, steamed

½ zucchini, julienned

½ bunch kale, lightly steamed and chopped

125g (4oz) baby spinach leaves

1 avocado, diced

METHOD

1. In a small serving sauce bowl, combine the tamari, chilli seasoning, honey, toasted sesame oil, and rice vinegar. Mix well and set aside.

2. Place cucumber slices in a small bowl. Sprinkle with half a teaspoon of salt and cover with water. Set aside to soften for 15 minutes.

3. Cook the rice according to the instructions on the packet. Drain and return to the pan, covered, to keep warm.

4. Heat oil in a medium saucepan and fry 2 eggs.

5. Bring a large saucepan of water to the boil. When boiling, add broccoli and cook for 3-5 minutes until tender. Remove with a slotted spoon and cover to keep warm. Add zucchini and cook for 3 minutes, until tender. Remove with a slotted spoon and cover to keep warm. Add kale and cook for 30 seconds. Drain.

6. Place rice in 2 individual serving bowls and top with the vegetables and fried egg. Pour over the sauce and serve.

SERVES 2 ★ PREP 20MIN ★ COOK TIME 1HR 30MIN

THYME POTATO GRATIN

INGREDIENTS

4 potatoes, thinly sliced

1 onion, sliced into rings

2 tsps fresh thyme

Salt and pepper, to taste

3 tbsps butter

3 tbsps plain flour

½ tsp salt

2 cups (500ml, 1pt) milk

1½ cup (190g, 6oz)
Cheddar cheese, grated

METHOD

1. Preheat oven to 200°C (400°F, Gas Mark 6). Butter a casserole dish.

2. Layer half of the potatoes into bottom of the prepared casserole dish. Top with onion slices and thyme, and then add the remaining potatoes. Season with salt and pepper to taste.

3. In a medium-size saucepan, melt butter over medium heat. Mix in the flour and salt, and stir constantly with a whisk or wooden spoon for one minute. Stir in milk. Cook, stirring constantly, until mixture has thickened. Add cheese at once, and continue stirring for 1 minute, until melted. Pour cheese sauce over the potatoes, and cover the dish with aluminum foil.

4. Place in oven and bake 1 hour. Remove aluminum foil and replace for a futher 15 minutes until a golden crust forms.

SPICED CAULIFLOWER AND BROCCOLI

INGREDIENTS

2 tbsps melted butter or ghee

1 tsp curry powder

½ tsp salt

Pinch of pepper

120g (4oz) cauliflower florets

120g (4oz) broccoli florets

½ cup (60g, 2oz) cashew nuts

Baby basil, to garnish

METHOD

1. Preheat the oven to 200°C (400°F, Gas Mark 6). Prepare a baking tray lined with greaseproof paper.

2. Mix the melted butter or ghee, curry powder, salt and pepper together in a mixing bowl. Add the cauliflower and broccoli.

3. Transfer the cauliflower and broccoli to baking tray arranging in one single layer. Roast for 15 minutes. Remove from the oven scatter with cashew nuts. Return to the oven to cook for a further 5 minutes.

4. Serve hot, garnished with basil.

BUTTERED MILLET WITH LEMON ROASTED ZUCCHINI

INGREDIENTS

Millet

1 tsp salt

3 tbsps butter, divided

1 cup (200g, 7oz) hulled millet

2 cups (500ml, 1pt) cold water

Roast zucchini

3 zucchini

1 clove garlic, finely chopped

2 lemons, halved

Olive oil, for drizzling

To serve

¼ cup (50g, 2oz) pepitas

¼ cup (50g, 2oz) sunflower seeds

125g (4oz) feta cheese, crumbled

10-12 mint leaves, to garnish

METHOD

1. Preheat oven to 200°C (400°F, Gas Mark 6).

2. Heat 2 tablespoons of butter in a saucepan over medium-high heat. Add millet and fry, stirring often, for a minute or so, until toasted. Add cold water and a pinch of salt and bring to the boil. Reduce heat to low and cover. Cook for 20 minutes. Remove from the heat and set aside for 5 minutes before adding 1 tablespoon of butter and fluffing with a fork.

3. Thinly slice zucchini and arrange in one layer on a shallow oven dish. Dot garlic over the zucchini and place lemon halves, flat side down, on the tray. Drizzle with oil and season with salt and pepper.

4. Roast for 10 minutes, turning zucchini over half way through, until soft and golden. Remove from oven and set aside to cool.

5. Meanwhile, toast pepitas and sunflower seeds in a dry frying pan over a medium-high heat for 2-3 minutes until aromatic and golden.

6. Gently squeeze the juice from the lemon halves into the oven dish. Add the millet and stir to combine zucchini, pan juices and lemon juice.

7. Serve buttered millet in bowls topped with feta cheese, toasted seeds and mint leaves.

TZATZIKI

INGREDIENTS

½ cucumber, peeled and finely diced

450g (1lb) plain Greek yoghurt

½ lemon, juiced

4 cloves garlic, crushed

½ cup (20g, ¾ oz) dill, chopped

½ tsp salt

Pinch of pepper

METHOD

1. Place cucumber in a sieve or cheesecloth and drain for 1 hour to remove excess water.

2. Combine the strained cucumber with yoghurt, lemon juice, garlic, dill, salt and pepper in a small bowl. Season to taste.

3. Refrigerate for 1 hour before serving.

SUMMER KEBABS

METHOD

1. Preheat oven to 200°C (400°F, Gas Mark 6).

2. Combine olive oil, garlic, lemon juice, mixed herbs, salt and pepper in a small bowl and whisk.

3. Thread eggplant, tomatoes, capsicums and zucchini onto skewers.

4. Place skewers onto a baking sheet. Brush olive oil mixture onto the skewers and let sit for 10-15 minutes.

5. Place into oven and roast for 10 minutes, or until tender.

6. Serve immediately, garnished with flat leaf parsley.

INGREDIENTS

Marinade

¼ cup (60ml, 2fl oz) olive oil

3 cloves garlic, crushed

1 lemon, juiced

½ tsp dried oregano

½ tsp dried basil

½ tsp salt

⅛ tsp pepper

Kebabs

1 Lebanese eggplant, cut into chunks

4 cherry tomatoes, halved

1 yellow capsicum, cut into chunks

1 red capsicum, cut into chunks

1 zucchini, sliced into thick rounds, halved

Flat leaf parsley, to garnish

MINI CHICKPEA CASSEROLES

INGREDIENTS

2 x 400g (14oz) cans chickpeas, drained and rinsed

1 cup (165g, 6oz) cooked brown rice

2 spring onions, sliced

1 lemon, juiced and zested

2 cloves garlic, minced

Salt and pepper, to season

2 eggs, beaten

1 cup (250ml, 8fl oz) cottage cheese

¾ cup (185ml, 6fl oz) plain yoghurt

1 cup (125g, 4oz) grated Parmesan cheese, divided

½ cup (20g, ¾ oz) fresh flat leaf parsley, chopped

½ cup (20g, ¾ oz) fresh oregano, chopped

4 cups (360g, 12oz) cauliflower rice (see page 154)

3 tbsps olive oil

Spiced roasted chickpeas and pecan nuts, to serve (optional)

METHOD

1. Preheat the oven to 190°C (375°F, Gas Mark 5) and lightly grease 6 individual ramekins.

2. In a large bowl, mix the chickpeas with the rice, spring onions, garlic, and lemon zest and juice. Season with salt and pepper.

3. Pour the eggs into a medium-sized bowl, then add cottage cheese, yoghurt, and half of the Parmesan cheese.

4. Stir the cottage cheese mixture into the chickpea mixture. Add the fresh herbs and stir to combine.

5. Spread the mixture in the prepared baking dishes.

6. Spoon cauliflower rice on top and sprinkle over the remaining half of the Parmesan cheese. Drizzle with olive oil.

7. Place in the oven and bake for 45 minutes, or until bubbling and golden. Remove and set aside to cool for 5 minutes before serving.

8. Serve hot with spiced roasted chickpeas and pecans, if desired.

SERVES 6 ★ PREP 20MIN ★ COOK TIME 30MIN
TUSCAN STEW

INGREDIENTS

Olive oil, for frying

1 onion, diced

1 carrot, diced

1 stick celery, diced

4 medium cloves garlic, minced

1 tsp dried thyme

¼ tsp red chilli flakes

½ tsp salt

¼ tsp pepper

1 x 400g (14oz) can cannellini beans, drained and rinsed

1 x 400g (14oz) can kidney beans, drained and rinsed

1 x 400g (14oz) can butter beans, drained and rinsed

2 cups (500ml, 1pt) vegetable stock

2 sprigs rosemary, leaves picked

2 bay leaves

8 cherry tomatoes

1 small bunch kale, tough stems removed, roughly chopped

Red onion slices, to garnish

METHOD

1. Heat the olive oil in a large saucepan over medium heat. Add the onion, carrot, and celery and cook, stirring occasionally for 5 minutes, until softened. Add the garlic and cook, stirring, for 1 minute. Stir in the thyme, chilli flakes, salt, and black pepper. Add the beans, stock, rosemary and bay leaves. Stir to combine.

2. Increase heat to medium-high and bring to a boil then reduce heat to low and cook on a gentle simmer for 20-25 minutes until thickened.

3. Add the tomatoes and kale and cook for 5 minutes, until kale is wilted.

4. Remove the bay leaves. Season to taste with salt and pepper.

5. Garnish with red onion slices.

VEGETABLE CURRY

INGREDIENTS

1 medium head cauliflower, broken into florets

2 tsps brown mustard seeds

2 tbsps vegetable oil

2 onions, sliced

2 carrots, quartered

2 garlic cloves, crushed

2 tsps grated fresh ginger

1 tsp ground turmeric

½ tsp chilli powder

1 tsp ground cumin

1 tsp garam masala

2 potatoes, diced

170g (6oz) green beans, trimmed

220g (8oz) plain Greek yoghurt

Sprig of mint, to garnish

METHOD

1. Bring a large pot of salted water to boil. Blanch the cauliflower until just tender, 4 minutes. Drain.

2. Heat a large saucepan over medium-high heat. Add mustard seeds and cook until they start to pop. Add the oil, onion, carrots, garlic and ginger and fry over medium heat for 5 minutes, or until the onion is soft.

3. Add the turmeric, chilli powder, cumin, garam marsala and potatoes and cook for 1-2 minutes, stirring to coat the potatoes with the spices.

4. Add ½ cup (125ml, 4fl oz) water and bring to the boil. Reduce the heat to medium-low, cover and simmer for 15 minutes, or until the potato is just tender and the liquid has absorbed. Add green beans and cauliflower and cook for a further 5 minutes.

5. Stir in the yoghurt and cook for 2-3 minutes until warmed through. Serve, garnished with mint.

SERVES 4 ★ PREP 20min ★ COOK TIME 1hr 40min

QUINOA ROASTED CAPSICUM WITH VINE TOMATOES

INGREDIENTS

Olive oil, for frying

1 onion, finely chopped

2 stalks celery,
finely chopped

1 tbsp ground cumin

2 cloves garlic, minced

300g cherry tomatoes
on the vine, one or two
sprigs reserved for
roasting

¾ cup (150g, 5oz) quinoa

1 carrot, grated

1 cup (125g, 4oz)
cheddar cheese, grated

1 tbsp dried mixed herbs

Salt and pepper, to taste

3 red capsicums, halved
lengthwise, ribs removed

¼ cup (30g, 1oz)
mozzarella cheese, grated

METHOD

1. Heat oil in a saucepan over medium heat. Add onion and celery, and cook for 7-8 minutes, or until soft. Add cumin and garlic, and fry for 1 minute.

2. Stir in cherry tomatoes, quinoa, carrot, and 2 cups water. Cover, and bring to a boil. Reduce heat to medium-low, and simmer for 15 minutes, or until quinoa is tender. Stir in cheddar cheese and mixed herbs. Season to taste with salt and pepper.

3. Preheat oven to 180°C (350°F, Gas Mark 4).

4. Fill each capsicum half with quinoa mixture, and place in baking tray. Place 2-3 tomato vines in the tray. Cover with foil, and bake for 1 hour.

5. Sprinkle mozarella cheese over the top of the capsicum and return to the oven to bake for a further 15 minutes, until tops are browned. Let stand 5 minutes. Transfer to serving plates, and drizzle with pan juices before serving.

CAULIFLOWER RICE

INGREDIENTS

1 cauliflower head,
stem and leaves removed

1 tbsp sesame oil

¼ tsp pepper

Vegetable oil, for frying

1 spring onion, thinly
sliced

Basil, to garnish

METHOD

1. Pulse cauliflower florets for 3 minutes in a food processor until it looks likes rice. Set aside.

2. Heat vegetable oil in a large frying pan or wok over a medium heat. Add spring onion and saute for 2-3 minutes.

3. Stir in cauliflower and cook for 3 minutes.

4. Serve warm, garnished with basil.

SERVES 6 ★ PREP 20MIN ★ COOK TIME 1HR 45MIN

ROSEMARY RATATOUILLE

INGREDIENTS

Olive oil, for frying

2 eggplants, diced

3 garlic cloves, finely chopped

Salt and pepper, to season

2 green zucchini, diced

2 yellow zucchini, diced

3-4 sprigs rosemary, leaves picked and chopped

1 onion, diced

2 red capsicum, diced

1kg (2lb) tomatoes, seeded and diced

2 cups (500ml, 1pt) tomato juice

METHOD

1. Heat the olive oil in a frying pan over low heat and add the eggplant and one-third of the garlic. Season with salt and pepper and fry, stirring, for 5 minutes, or until tender. Transfer eggplant to a large saucepan.

2. Return the pan to the heat and add more oil. Add the zucchini, another third of the garlic, half the rosemary and some salt and pepper. Saute for 3-4 minutes, until tender, then add to the saucepan with the eggplant.

3. Add more oil to the pan and saute the onion, capsicum and remaining garlic and rosemary for 5 minutes, until tender.

4. Combine all the cooked vegetables in a pot. Add the tomatoes and simmer on a very low heat for 1½ hours. Remove from the heat, taste for seasoning and serve garnished with rosemary.

RISOTTO STUFFED TOMATOES

INGREDIENTS

2 tbsps olive oil, divided

1 small onion, finely chopped

½ clove garlic, minced

⅔ cup (100g, 4oz) Arborio rice

¼ cup (60ml, 2fl oz) dry white wine

1¼ cups (310ml, 10fl oz) vegetable stock (warm)

½ tbsp capers, finely chopped

1½ tbsps Parmesan cheese, grated

½ cup (20g, ¾ oz) fresh parsley, chopped

6 large tomatoes

METHOD

1. Heat the oil in a large deep-sided frying pan or saucepan over a medium-high heat. Add the onion and garlic and cook, stirring, for 3-5 minutes until soft

2. Add the rice and toast for a few minutes, until translucent. Pour in the white wine and allow to evapourate.

3. Add the vegetable stock, a ladle at a time, stirring constantly. Cook for 20 minutes, until the risotto is creamy but rice is just cooked. Add the capers, Parmesan cheese and parsley and mix well.

4. Preheat the oven to 180°C (350°F, Gas Mark 4) and grease an ovenproof dish.

5. Use a sharp knife to cut off the top of the tomatoes and keep them as lids. Scoop out the pulp and discard.

6. Place the tomato shells into the ovenproof dish and fill each with the risotto. Place the lids on top of each tomato, and drizzle the remaining olive oil on top.

7. Place in the oven and bake for about 20 minutes or until the tomatoes are soft.

GARLIC TOFU STIRFRY

INGREDIENTS

450g (1lb) extra firm tofu

Sauce

¼ cup (60ml, 2fl oz) soy sauce

2 tbsps rice vinegar

2 tbsps maple syrup

2 tbsps water

4 garlic cloves, minced

2 tsps cornflour

Stir fry

Sesame oil, for frying

4 dried chilli peppers, halved (optional)

Sesame seeds and fresh parsley, chopped, to garnish

Steamed broccolini, to serve

METHOD

1. Slice the tofu and then place it out flat on a baking tray or chopping board covered in paper towels. Place another plate on top. Press for 15 minutes. Allow the water to absorb and replace towels if needed.

2. Meanwhile, place the sauce ingredients together in a small bowl and whisk to combine. Set aside.

3. After 15 minutes, pat tofu dry and chop into small cubes.

4. Heat 1 tbsp of oil in a large frying pan over medium heat. Add tofu cubes in a single layer. Cook for 10 minutes, turning occasionally during cooking to brown all sides. Add chilli peppers, if using, half way through cooking.

5. Garnish with sesame seeds and chopped parsley, and serve with broccolini.

BARLEY MUSHROOM RISOTTO

INGREDIENTS

Olive oil, for frying

1 onion, finely chopped

2 tbsps butter

225g (8oz, ½ lb)
cremini mushrooms
(or button mushrooms),
quartered

3 cups (750ml, 24fl oz)
vegetable stock

1 cup (155g, 4oz)
pearl barley

1 tsp salt

fresh flat leaf parsley,
to garnish

METHOD

1. Heat the oil in a saucepaon over a medium-high heat. Add onion and fry, stirring, for 5 minutes until translucent.

2. Meanwhile heat the butter in a large frying pan over a medium-high heat. Add mushrooms and cook, stirring, for 5 minutes until tender.

3. Add stock, barley and salt to the saucepan with the onion and bring to a boil. Partially cover pan and reduce heat to low. Simmer for 1 hour, stirring occasionally, until barley is tender.

4. Mix mushrooms through the barley and serve, garnished with fresh parsley.

SERVES 2 ★ PREP 20MIN ★ COOK TIME 4MIN

KALE AND SPROUT SALAD WITH TOASTED ALMONDS

INGREDIENTS

Lemon dressing

2 tbsps Dijon mustard

1 lemon, juiced and zested

2 tsps honey

¼ cup (60ml, 2fl oz) olive oil

2 tsps flax seeds

Salad

1 bunch kale, tough stems removed and chopped

150g (5oz) Brussels sprouts

3 tbsps slivered almonds

¼ cup (30g, 1oz) Parmesan cheese, finely grated

METHOD

1. Place the ingredients for the dressing in a small bowl and mix well to combine. Set aside.
2. Remove the stems and any discoloured outer leaves from the sprouts using a sharp knife. Cut the sprouts into halves or quarters depending on their size. Place sprouts and kale into a serving bowl.
3. Place the almond slivers in a small frying pan over medium heat and cook, stirring, for 3-4 minutes until golden.
4. Add the toasted almonds and Parmesan cheese to the salad and stir to combine.
5. When ready to serve, pour over the dressing and toss to coat the salad.

STUFFED BAKED ZUCCHINI

INGREDIENTS

4 large zucchini

1 tbsp vegetable oil

1 onion, chopped

½ red capsicum, chopped

½ green capsicum, chopped

2 garlic cloves, minced

1 carrot, grated

¾ cup (120g, 4oz) frozen peas, cooked

1 cup (165g, 6oz) cooked couscous

Salt and pepper, to taste

1 cup (125g, 4oz) mozzarella cheese, grated

METHOD

1. Preheat the oven to 190°C (375°F, Gas Mark 5) and line a baking tray.

2. Cut the zucchinis in half lengthwise. Scoop out the insides, leaving a border all the way around. Place zucchini shells on the baking tray. Chop the zucchini flesh and set aside.

3. Heat the oil in a large frying pan over a medium-high heat. Add onion, capsicum and garlic and cook for 6-8 minutes until soft. Add the zucchini flesh, carrot, peas and cook until heated through.

4. Remove from heat and stir in the cooked couscous. Add salt and pepper to taste. Spoon mixture into the zucchini shells and cover with grated cheese.

5. Place in the oven and bake for 25 minutes until cheese has melted.

SERVES 4 ★ PREP 20MIN ★ COOK TIME 1HR

THREE CHEESE SOUFFLE

INGREDIENTS

1 tbsp butter, softened

7 large eggs

115g (4oz) sour cream

⅓ cup (80ml, 3fl oz) milk

¼ tsp pepper

1 tsp dry mustard

¼ tsp ground nutmeg

30g (1oz) cheddar cheese, grated

30g (1oz) Harvati cheese, grated

30g (1oz) Gruyere cheese, grated

METHOD

1. Preheat the oven to 180°C (350°F, Gas Mark 4), and brush butter over the inside of the souffle dish.

2. Using an electric mixer, blend together the eggs, sour cream and milk for 30 seconds. Add pepper, dry mustard and nutmeg and whisk to combine.

3. Layer the cheese in the soufflé dish, then pour the egg mixture gently over the top.

4. Place the soufflé in the oven and bake for 1 hour, until golden and well risen.

5. Serve immediately.

SERVES 4 ★ PREP 15MIN ★ COOK TIME 30MIN

QUINOA PECAN PILAF

INGREDIENTS

1 cup (170g, 6oz) quinoa, rinsed

1¾ cups (440ml, 15fl oz) vegetable stock

Olive oil, for frying

1 onion, finely chopped

¾ tsp dried thyme

150g (5oz) shiitake mushrooms, thinly sliced

2 cloves garlic, minced

¼ tsp salt

1/8 tsp pepper

½ cup (60g, 2oz) pecans, toasted and chopped

Cheddar cheese, grated, to serve

METHOD

1. Combine quinoa and stock in a medium saucepan. Bring to a boil, then turn heat down to low, cover and simmer for 15 minutes until quinoa is tender.

2. In the meantime, heat olive oil in a large saucepan over medium heat. Add the onion and cook for 3 minutes, stirring occasionally, until it starts to soften. Add the thyme and cook, stirring occasionally, for 2 minutes.

3. Refresh the pan with more olive oil, then add mushrooms and garlic. Cook for 3 minutes more, stirring constantly, until mushrooms are cooked. Add salt and pepper.

4. Add quinoa and pecans to the pan and stir well to combine.

5. Serve in bowls garnished with grated cheese.

PICO DE GALLO

INGREDIENTS

750g (1½lb) ripe
tomatoes, diced

1 tsp salt

½ large onion, diced

2 jalapeño chillies,
finely diced

½ cup (20g, ¾ oz)
coriander leaves, finely
chopped

1 tbsp lime juice

METHOD

1. Place tomatoes in a large bowl and sprinkle over salt. Toss to
   combine, then transfer to a mesh strainer or colander set over a
   bowl and allow to drain for 30 minutes. Discard liquid.

2. Combine drained tomatoes with onion, chillies, coriander and lime
   juice. Toss to combine and season to taste with salt.

BAKED ARTICHOKE

INGREDIENTS

4-5 artichokes

3 tbsps butter

2 tsps garlic, crushed

2 tsps fresh lemon juice

Handful of fresh sage

Handful of fresh thyme

½ tsp salt

2 cups (340g, 12oz) peas, steamed

Lemon slices

METHOD

1. Preheat oven to 220°C (425°F, Gas Mark 7) and prepare a baking tray with baking paper.

2. Cut the stem of each artichoke so that about an inch remains. Using scissors snip the tips off the leaves. Slice the artichoke in half. Using a small paring knife, slice out the choke, both the white part and very inner purple leaves.

3. Melt butter in a saucepan over low heat. Add garlic and lemon and mix.

4. Place the artichokes face up on a baking sheet, along with sage and thyme and season with salt.

5. Using a spoon, drizzle the artichokes with the butter mixture, making sure to get in-between the leaves.

6. Roast in oven for 35-45 minutes until tender.

7. Serve with steamed peas and lemon slices.

ASIAN-STYLE VEGETABLE BURGER

INGREDIENTS

Olive oil, for frying

1 onion, chopped

1 garlic clove, crushed

2 zucchini, grated

2 carrots, grated

4 slices bread, crusts removed

1 x 400g (14oz) can chickpeas, rinsed and drained

3 tsps curry paste

3 tbsps crunchy peanut butter

½ tsp cumin

1 egg yolk

¼ cup (10g, ¼ oz) coriander leaves, chopped

6 bread rolls

6-8 lettuce leaves

10 white radishes, julienned

80g (3oz) snow pea shoots (or rocket leaves)

METHOD

1. Heat oil in a large frying pan over medium-low heat. Add the onion and cook for 5 minutes, until softened. Add garlic, zucchini and carrot, and cook, stirring, for 3 minutes until softened. Drain off excess liquid.

2. Place bread and chickpeas in the bowl of a food processor and pulse to combine. Add vegetables, curry paste, peanut butter, cumin, egg yolk and coriander. Process until mixture comes together.

3. Form the mixture into 6 patties. Place in the refrigerator to chill for 15 minutes.

4. Heat the oil in a large frying pan over medium heat and cook the burgers, in batches, for 2 minutes each side until golden.

5. Open the bread rolls and line the bottom half with butter lettuce and sliced radish. Add the patty and then top with rocket. Gently press the top half of the bun over the rocket. Fix in place with a toothpick, if necessary.

RED CABBAGE WITH APPLES

INGREDIENTS

1 medium red cabbage, thinly shredded

1 onion, thinly sliced

3 apples, peeled, cored and thinly sliced

4 tbsps balsamic vinegar

3 tbsps water

2-3 tbsps olive oil

Salt and pepper to taste

fresh rosemary, to garnish

METHOD

1. Preheat the oven to 180°C (350°F, Gas Mark 4).

2. Mix all the ingredients in a large baking tray, spreading out evenly across the base. Loosely cover with foil.

3. Transfer to the oven to bake. After 60 minutes, check the cabbage, stir and taste. Cover and cook for a further 30 minutes, if required, until the cabbage is tender, juicy and sweet.

4. Season with sea salt and freshly ground black pepper and garnish with fresh rosemary to serve.

SERVES 4 ★ PREP 10MIN ★ COOK TIME 15MIN

EASY PALAK PANEER

INGREDIENTS

900g (2lb) spinach

Salt, to taste

2-3 green chillies

3 tbsps oil

½ tsp cumin seeds

8-10 garlic cloves, finely chopped

200g (7oz) paneer, cubed

1 tbsp lemon juice

4 tbsps fresh cream

METHOD

1. Remove stems and wash spinach thoroughly in running water. Blanch in salted boiling water for 2 minutes. Refresh in chilled water. Squeeze out excess water.

2. Place spinach and green chillies in a blender or food processer and grind into a fine paste.

3. Heat oil in a frying pan on a meduim heat. Add the cumin seeds. When they begin to darken, add garlic and saute for half a minute. Add the spinach puree and stir.Check seasoning.

4. Add water if required. When the gravy comes to a boil, add the paneer and mix well. Stir in lemon juice.

5. Before serving stir in fresh cream. Serve hot with naan bread.

SESAME TOFU BURGER

INGREDIENTS

Marinade

¼ cup (60ml, 2fl oz) toasted sesame oil

⅓ cup (80ml, 3fl oz) soy sauce

2 tbsps lemon juice

Small piece ginger, finely grated

1-2 cloves garlic, minced

Burger

3 tbsps toasted sesame seeds

450g (1lb) firm or extra firm tofu, drained

1 red capsicum, thickly sliced

2 zucchini, sliced lengthwise

3-4 mushrooms, sliced

½ onion, sliced

To serve

6 ciabatta buns

Butter lettuce leaves

Raw carrot, julienned

Fresh chives

Pumpkin seeds

Tomato salsa

METHOD

1. Place marinade ingredients in a small bowl and whisk to combine.

2. Scatter toasted sesame seeds on a plate.

3. Cut tofu into 6 slices. Pat each square dry with paper towels. Place tofu slices in a shallow dish and pour over marinade. Cover and refrigerate for 1 hour.

4. Preheat grill to a medium heat.

5. Remove tofu from dish, retaining marinade. Place tofu slices on an oiled grill rack and grill for 3 minutes on each side. Brush tofu with the reserved marinade and then roll both sides in the toasted sesame seeds.

6. Place capsicum, zucchini, mushroom and onion slices on grill rack and grill for 3-4 minutes each side, until blistered.

7. Build the burger on a ciabatta bun using the salad ingredients, roasted vegetables, pumpkin seeds and tomato salsa.

DEEP FRIED TOFU

INGREDIENTS

Soy-ginger dressing

Medium piece ginger, minced

½ cup (125ml, 4fl oz) soy sauce

2 tbsps sesame oil

1 tsp sugar

455g (1lb) firm tofu

3 tbsps cornflour

Oil for deep frying, as needed

METHOD

1. Place all the ingredients for the dressing into a small bowl and mix well to combine.

2. Drain the tofu.

3. Cut the tofu into 4 large rectangles.

4. Roll the tofu in the cornflour.

5. Heat enough oil for deep frying in a wok over a high heat.

6. Fry, stirring occasionally, until the tofu is golden on both sides. Remove with a slotted spoon and drain on paper towels. Keep warm while frying the remaining tofu.

7. Serve with soy-ginger dressing or sweet and sour sauce (opposite).

SERVES 4 ★ PREP 5MIN ★ COOK TIME 10MIN

SWEET AND SOUR SAUCE

INGREDIENTS

¾ cup (120g, 4oz) brown sugar

1 tbsp cornflour

1 x 225g (8oz) can of pineapple pieces with juice

$1/3$ cup (80ml, 3fl oz) vinegar

$1/3$ cup (80ml, 3fl oz) water

1 tbsp soy sauce

½ red capsicum, chopped

METHOD

1. Combine the brown sugar, cornflour, pineapple, vinegar, water and soy sauce in a medium-sized saucepan over a medium-high heat.

2. Bring to a boil, stirring constantly. Reduce heat to a simmer and cover. Simmer for 5 minutes, stirring occasionally.

3. Stir in capsicum and simmer for a further 2-3 minutes, until desired thickness is reached.

VEGAN

MUNG BEAN CURRY

INGREDIENTS

2 potatoes, peeled and quartered

1 tsp coconut oil

1 large onion, finely chopped

6 garlic cloves, crushed

2 tsps brown mustard seeds

1 tsp turmeric

½ tsp ground coriander

1 tsp curry powder

1 tsp cumin

½ tsp chilli flakes (optional)

1¼ tsps salt

1 x 400ml (14fl oz) can coconut milk

3 cups (750ml, 24fl oz) boiling water

1 cup (200g, 7oz) mung beans

Sprig of mint, to garnish

METHOD

1. Place potatoes in a pan of water and bring to the boil. Cook for 15 minutes until fork tender. Drain and return potatoes to the pan. Mash with a potato masher or fork.

2. Heat oil in a saucepan on low-medium heat. Add onion and cook, stirring occasionally, until golden brown, approximately 5 minutes. Add garlic and fry for 1-2 minutes until the strong aroma disappears. Next add the brown mustard seeds and cook for a minute or two until they pop. Then add turmeric, coriander, curry powder, cumin, chilli flakes, if using, and salt and cook for another 30 seconds, stirring frequently.

3. Pour in the coconut milk, mashed potato, water and mung beans and stir to combine. Bring to a boil, cover and cook on a low heat for 45 minutes. Remove from heat and let stand 5 minutes before serving, garnished with mint.

SERVES 3 ★ PREP 15MIN ★ COOK TIME 15MIN

AGEDASHI TOFU

INGREDIENTS

1 block (400g, 14 oz) silken tofu

4 tbsps potato starch

Vegetable oil, for frying

Sauce

1 cup (250ml, 8fl oz) kombu dashi

2 tbsps tamari (or soy sauce)

2 tbsps mirin

Toppings

1 tbsp ginger, finely grated, to garnish

2 tsps chives, finely chopped

METHOD

1. Wrap the tofu in 3-4 layers of paper towels and place on a plate. Place a flat plate on top of the tofu and leave for 15 minutes. Drain off any excess liquid and discard paper towels. Pat tofu dry with clean paper towels.

2. Cut tofu into 8 pieces and roll each piece in potato starch to coat well.

3. Put kombu dashi, tamari, and mirin in a saucepan and bring to a boil. Turn off the heat and set aside.

4. Heat the oil in a large frying pan and deep fry tofu until light brown and crispy.

5. Remove the tofu and drain excess oil on a plate lined with paper towels.

6. To serve, place the tofu in a serving bowl and pour the sauce around the tofu. Garnish with grated ginger and chives.

SERVES 4 ★ PREP 20MIN ★ COOK TIME 35MIN

EGGPLANT AND WHITE BEAN BALLS

INGREDIENTS

Olive oil, for frying

1 eggplant, diced

½ tsp black pepper

1 onion, finely chopped

⅛ tsp cayenne pepper

2 cloves garlic, minced

2 cups (370g, 12oz)
cooked cannellini beans

¼ cup (10g, ¼ oz)
flat leaf parsley, chopped

Pinch of red chilli flakes

¾ cup (90g, 3oz)
breadcrumbs

¼ tsp salt

METHOD

1. Preheat oven to 190°C (375°F, Gas Mark 5) and line a baking tray.

2. Heat a tablespoon of oil in a frying pan and saute eggplant for 5 minutes over a medium heat. Add more oil if required to prevent sticking.

3. Season with salt and pepper.

4. Add water to just cover the eggplant. Cook for 15 minutes, until tender. Set aside.

5. Heat a tablespoon of oil in the same pan. Add onion, cayenne pepper and garlic and saute for 5 minutes, until soft.

6. Pulse eggplant, beans, parsley, chilli and the onion mixture in a food processor until well combined.

7. Add to a bowl with breadcrumbs and mix with hands until well combined.

8. Form small balls from the mixture and place on baking tray.

9. Bake for 15 minutes. Turn off oven and let cook for a further 20 minutes, until heated though and golden.

10. Serve on rice with tomato sauce. Garnish with parsley.

SPICY CURRY PATTIES

INGREDIENTS

1 x 400g (14oz) can
chickpeas, drained
and rinsed

½ red onion, finely diced

1 zucchini, grated

3 tbsps coriander,
finely chopped

3 tbsps red wine vinegar

2 cloves garlic, minced

2 tbsps peanut butter

1 tsp cumin

½ tsp tumeric

1 tsp garlic powder

2 tsps black pepper

½ tsp sea salt

1 cup (190g, 7oz)
cooked red quinoa

1 bunch spinach,
leaves picked

2 tbsps olive oil

METHOD

1. Place the chickpeas in a large bowl and mash with a fork.

2. Add all the other ingredients to the bowl and mix well
    to combine.

3. Using your hands, form into 6 patties of equal size.

4. Heat the oil in a frying pan over a medium-high heat and fry patties,
    two at a time, for 3 minutes each side until crisp and golden.

LENTIL FRITTERS

INGREDIENTS

1 cup (125g, 4oz) self-raising flour

½ cup (100g, 3½ oz) milk

2 eggs

1 x 400g (14oz) can of brown or green lentils, drained and rinsed

1 x 310g (11oz) can corn kernels, drained and rinsed

½ red capsicum, diced

2 spring onions, finely sliced

Olive oil, for frying

METHOD

1. Sift flour over a large mixing bowl.

2. Whisk milk and eggs together. Slowly add milk mixture to the flour and stir well to combine.

3. Add lentils, corn, capsicum, and spring onions to the batter.

4. Heat olive oil in a large frying pan over medium-high heat. Drop a heaped tablespoon of batter into the pan for each fritter. Flatten with a spatula and cook for 2 minutes until golden brown. Flip and cook on the other side for a further 2 minutes.

SERVES 4 ★ PREP 15MIN ★ COOK TIME 1HR 45MIN

STUFFED CABBAGE ROLLS WITH RICE AND MUSHROOMS

INGREDIENTS

1 cup (155g, 4oz) wild rice (or brown rice)

1 tsp olive oil

1 onion, finely chopped

3 cloves garlic, minced

225g (8oz, ½ lb) mushrooms, finely chopped

Pinch of chilli flakes

2 tsps thyme

¼ tsp pepper

½ tsp salt

1 head savoy cabbage, leaves removed

Sauce

400g (14oz) passata

⅓ cup (80ml, 3fl oz) tomato paste

2 tsps basil

½ tsp salt

½ tsp smoked paprika

1 cup (250ml, 8fl oz) water

fresh parsley, chopped, for garnish

METHOD

1. Cook the rice according to the instructions on the packet.

2. Heat the oil in a large frying pan over medium heat. Add the onion and saute for 5 minutes until translucent. Add the garlic, mushrooms, chilli flakes, thyme, pepper, and salt. Saute for 5 minutes, until the mushrooms are cooked. Add cooked rice and stir, then set aside.

3. Place all of the sauce ingredients in a saucepan over medium heat and bring to the boil. Immediately reduce heat, cover and simmer for 5 minutes. Set aside.

4. Place the cabbage leaves in a large bowl. Fill the bowl with boiling water and cover the bowl with a plate. Allow to sit for 10 minutes to soften the cabbage.

5. Preheat the oven to 180°C (350°F, Gas Mark 4).

6. Coat the base of a baking dish with a layer of the sauce.

7. Take a cabbage leaf and pat dry with kitchen paper. Place 2-3 tablespoons of the filling mixture at one end of the cabbage leaf. Roll up like a burrito, tucking in the sides. Continue rolling until all leaves are filled.

8. Place the rolled leaves side by side in the baking dish. Cover with the remaining sauce and place in the oven to bake for 45 minutes.

9. Serve garnished with fresh parsley.

CHICKPEA CURRY WITH BASMATI RICE

INGREDIENTS

1 tbsp olive oil

1 onion, chopped

3 garlic cloves, minced

Medium piece of ginger, finely chopped

1 eggplant, diced

1 red capsicum, diced

2 tsps garam masala

1 tsp cumin

¼ tsp cayenne pepper

1 x 400g (14oz) can chickpeas, drained and rinsed

2 x 400g (14oz) cans chopped tomatoes

Squeeze of fresh lemon

Basmati rice, for serving

METHOD

1. Heat olive oil in a large saucepan over medium-high heat. Add the onion and fry for 5 minutes, until translucent. Add the garlic and ginger and cook for a couple of minutes more, stirring frequently. Add the eggplant and capsicum and cook for 3-5 minutes until starting to soften.

2. Add the garam masala, cumin and cayenne pepper, and stir to coat with the spices. Cook for 1-2 minutes until spices are aromatic.

3. Add the chickpeas and stir well so they are covered in oil and spice. Add the tomatoes and stir, then reduce heat to medium-low and allow to simmer gently for 20 minutes.

4. At the end of cooking, add a squeeze of fresh lemon juice if desired. Serve with basmati rice.

VEGETABLE AND TOFU STIR FRY

INGREDIENTS

300g (10oz) hard tofu

300g (10oz) thin rice noodles

½ cup (100g, 3½ oz) vegetable stock

1 tbsp tamari (or soy sauce)

1 tbsp rice wine or dry sherry

2 tsps sesame oil

1 tbsp garlic, minced

Small piece ginger, minced

¼ tsp red chilli flakes

2 tbsps vegetable oil, for frying

1 large carrot, julienned

1 green capsicum, julienned

1 red capsicum, julienned

1 yellow capsicum, julienned

1 bunch baby bok choy

Salt, to taste

½ tsp sugar

METHOD

1. Slice the tofu and then place it out flat on a baking tray or chopping board covered in paper towels. Place another plate on top. Press for 15 minutes. Allow the water to absorb and replace towels if needed.

2. Place the noodles in a large bowl, and cover with warm water. Soak for at least 20 minutes, until soft. Set aside.

3. Whisk stock, tamari, rice wine and sesame oil together in a small bowl.

4. Combine the garlic, ginger and chilli flakes in another bowl.

5. Heat a large frying pan or wok over high heat. Slowly pour in vegetable oil. Add the tofu. Reduce the heat to medium-high, and stir-fry for 3 minutes until the tofu is golden brown. Add the garlic, ginger and chilli, and stir-fry for no more than 10 seconds. Add the carrot and capsicums and stir-fry for 3 minutes. Add the stock mixture, noodles, spring onions, buk choy, salt and sugar.

6. Stir-fry for 1-2 minutes until the noodles are just tender and the stock has been absorbed, then serve.

ONE-POT LENTIL AND MUSHROOM QUINOA

INGREDIENTS

2 tbsps olive oil

1 onion, chopped

2 carrots, chopped

8 button mushrooms, diced

3 garlic cloves, minced

½ tsp red chilli flakes

1 tsp dried oregano

2 tbsps fresh thyme

2 bay leaves

1 cup (185g, 6oz) red lentils

2 cups (500ml, 1pt) vegetable stock

2½ cups (625ml, 20fl oz) water

1 tsp miso paste

½ cup (100g, 3oz) red quinoa, uncooked

1 bunch spinach, leaves picked

Salt and pepper, to taste

Olive oil and chopped cashews, to garnish

METHOD

1. Heat the oil in a large saucepan over medium-high heat. Add onions and carrots and cook for 5 minutes, until the vegetables have started to soften, about 3-4 minutes. Add mushrooms and continue to cook for a further 5 minutes, until mushrooms are tender.

2. Add garlic, chilli flakes and herbs. Stir for 1-2 minutes until aromatic.

3. Add lentils, stock, water and miso and bring the mixture to a boil. Cover and reduce heat to a simmer for 15 minutes.

4. Add quinoa and stir to combine. Bring the mixture back to a boil, then reduce to simmer, covered, for a further 15 minutes.

5. Remove pot from the heat, and add spinach, stirring gently to combine. Season with salt and pepper to taste.

6. Serve with a drizzle of olive oil and chopped cashews.

SERVES 4 ★ PREP 15MIN ★ COOK TIME 30MIN

BAKED EGGPLANT AND QUINOA

INGREDIENTS

2 eggplants

1 tbsp olive oil

2 garlic cloves, finely chopped

¾ cup (150g, 5oz) quinoa

1½ cups (375ml, 13fl oz) vegetable stock

1 tsp salt

Pinch of pepper

½ cup (60g, 2oz) pine nuts

Fresh parsley, to garnish

METHOD

1. Preheat oven to 230°C (450°F, Gas Mark 8) and line a baking tray with greaseproof paper.

2. Place eggplants on the baking tray and transfer to oven. Bake for 15 minutes, until soft. Remove from the oven and allow to cool slightly.

3. Cut each eggplant in half lengthwise and scoop out the flesh, leaving a border so they hold their shape. Finely chop the eggplant flesh.

4. Meanwhile, heat oil in a large frying pan over medium-high heat. Add the garlic and cook, stirring, for about 1 minute until fragrant. Add the quinoa, stock, salt and and pepper and stir. Reduce the heat to low, cover, and cook for about 15 minutes, until quinoa is tender. Add pine nuts and eggplant flesh and stir to combine.

5. Divide the quinoa mixture equally among the 4 eggplant skins. Garnish with parsley and serve.

CANNELLINI BEAN DIP

INGREDIENTS

1 x 400g (14oz) can cannellini beans, drained and rinsed

2½ tbsps tahini

2 tbsps olive oil

1 lemon, juiced

1 clove garlic, crushed

½ tsp salt

2-3 tbsps water as needed

Handful parsley and lemon slices, to garnish

METHOD

1. Place all ingredients except water in a food processor and blend to a paste.

2. Add water one tablespoon at a time to thin to the desired consistency.

3. Garnish with chopped parsley and serve with lemon slices.

SERVES 4 ★ PREP 10MIN ★ COOK TIME 40MIN

BEETROOT PATTIES

INGREDIENTS

1 large beetroot

1 cup (100g, 4oz) cooked brown rice

200g (7oz) feta cheese crumbled

2 eggs, beaten

1 tsp cumin

2 tbsps dill, chopped

2 tbsps mint, chopped

½ cup (60g, 2oz) almond flour

2 tbsps olive oil

Green salad, to serve

METHOD

1. Place beetroot in a pan of water and bring to the boil. Reduce the heat and simmer for 40 minutes, until tender. Drain and set aside to cool.
2. Once cooled, slip the skins off the beetroot, then grate coarsely and put in to a bowl. Add the rice, feta cheese, eggs, cumin, herbs, almond flour and combine well.
3. Using your hand, shape into patties.
4. Heat the olive oil in a large frying pan over a medium-high heat until shimmering.Then reduce heat to medium and fry the patties. Cook for 2-3 minutes each side until crisp and warmed through.
5. Serve warm with green salad.

OKRA MASALA CURRY

INGREDIENTS

250g (9oz) okra, topped and tailed

Oil for frying

1 medium onion, coarsely chopped

1 tsp Sriracha ginger-garlic paste

2 medium tomatoes, chopped

1 tsp ground coriander

½ tsp chilli powder

½ tsp ground turmeric

½ tsp garam masala

½ tsp amchur (dry mango powder) (optional)

Salt, to taste

METHOD

1. Rinse the okra in water and then leave to dry or wipe with a kitchen towel.

2. Heat 2 tablespoons of the oil in a wok or large frying pan. Add okra and cook, stirring frequently, until tender and no longer crunchy, approximately 5-7 minutes. Set aside.

3. Heat 1 tablespoon oil on a medium-high heat and add onion. Fry until they are translucent, approximately 5 minutes. Add the ginger-garlic paste and saute for approximately 1 minute.

4. Add the chopped tomatoes and saute until soft. If the tomato mixture becomes too dry add water and continue cooking.

5. Add the dry spice powders, stir and saute for 1 minute.

6. Add the okra and mix so that the onion-tomato masala coats the okra well. Taste and season with salt as needed. Cook for a further 2-3 minutes and then serve.

VEGAN TACOS

INGREDIENTS

Spice Paste

2 tsps chilli powder

1 tsp cumin

1 tsp coriander

½ tsp onion powder

½ tsp sea salt

1 tbsp vegetable oil

To serve

455g (1lb) extra firm tofu, sliced lengthwise

6 soft corn tortillas

1 orange capsicum, sliced

1 red capsicum, sliced

3 spring onions, halved

Micro cress, to serve

METHOD

1. Preheat grill to a medium high setting.

2. Combine ingredients for the spice paste in a small bowl and stir well to combine. Rub the tofu with the spice paste on all sides.

3. Grill the slices for 3 minutes each side, until golden brown.

4. Place capsicum and spring onion on the grill for 2 minutes each side, until lightly charred and spring onion is wilted.

5. Layer each tortilla with tofu, capsicum, spring onion and top with micro cress.

VEGAN CHOCOLATE TART

INGREDIENTS

Crust

1 cup (125g, 4oz)
raw cashew nuts

¾ cup (60g, 2oz) almond
meal

½ cup (40g, 1½ oz)
unsweetened shredded
coconut

2½ tbsps cacao or
cocoa powder

6 dates, pitted and
chopped roughly

¼ tsp salt

Filling

1 ½ cup (185g, 6oz)
raw cashew nuts

½ cup (100g, 3½ oz)
coconut milk

½ cup (60g, 2oz) cacao
or cocoa powder

¼ cup (90g, 3oz) + 1 tbsp
rice malt syrup or maple
syrup

2 tbsps coconut oil

2 tsps vanilla extract

½ tsp salt

flaked almonds, to
garnish

METHOD

1. Place all raw cashews required for this recipe into a medium sized bowl. Fill with water, cover and soak overnight. In the morning, drain, rinse and divide into 1 cup and 1½ cup portions. Set aside.

2. Place cashew nuts into a food processor or high-speed blender, and pulse until a coarse crumb forms. Add the remaining ingredients for the crust, and continue to pulse until the mixture is well combined.

3. Press mixture evenly into baking tray. Damp hands will make this easier if the mixture is sticky.

4. Add the soaked raw cashew nuts along with all the other filling ingredients into a food processor or high-speed blender and mix until smooth.

5. Fill baking tray with chocolate filling and refrigerate for an hour or freeze for 30 minutes or until set.

6. Garnish with flaked almonds before serving.

RAW CARROT CAKE WITH CASHEW CREAM

INGREDIENTS

Cake

2 large carrots, diced

1½ cups (240g, 8oz) oat or buckwheat flour

1 cup (140g, 5oz) dates

1 cup (140g, 5oz) dried pineapple

½ cup (80g, 3oz) dried coconut

½ tsp cinnamon

Frosting

2 cups (280g, 10oz) cashews, soaked for 2 hours

1-2 tbsps lemon juice

2 tbsps coconut oil

⅓ cup (80ml, 3fl oz) maple syrup

Water, as needed

Cashew nuts and dried cranberries, chopped, to decorate

METHOD

1. Place all the cake ingredients in the food processor and pulse until coarsely chopped and a dough-like consistency forms. Set aside.

2. Place all the frosting ingredients in a high speed blender and blend until smooth, adding a small amount of water, just enough to hold the frosting together.

3. Press half the cake mix into the bottom of an adjustable spring-form pan. Then spread over a generous layer of the frosting. Put in the freezer for 30 minutes or until the layer of frosting is hard.

4. Remove from freezer and press on the rest of the cake mix. Remove cake from the tin. Spread remaining frosting on the top and sides of the cake. Scatter with cashews and cranberries. Refrigerate until ready to eat.

SNACKS AND SWEETS

SWEET POTATO SAMOSAS

INGREDIENTS

Pastry

1 cup (125g, 4oz) wholemeal plain flour

½ tsp salt

30g (1oz) butter, chilled

2-3 tbsps water

2 sweet potatoes, diced

2 tbsp vegetable oil

½ onion, finely chopped

Small piece ginger, minced

2 tsp curry powder

½ tsp salt

¼ tsp chili powder (optional)

1 tsp fresh lemon juice

Oil for frying

METHOD

1. Sift the flour and salt into a mixing bowl. Rub in the butter until the mixture resembles breadcrumbs. Add the water and knead thoroughly to form a smooth dough. Cover in plastic wrap and place in the fridge to chill while preparing the filling.

2. Place the potatoes, covered with water, in a saucepan over a high heat and bring to the boil. Boil for 20 minutes until cooked. Drain. Set aside.

3. Heat the vegetable oil in a large frying pan over medium heat. Add the onion, ginger, curry powder and chilli powder, if using. Cook, stirring, for 5 minutes until the onions soften. Add the potatoes and stir to coat with the spices. Cook, stirring, for 2-3 minutes and remove from heat when potatoes begin to brown. Add the lemon juice and salt and stir. Set aside to cool.

4. Divide the pastry into 8 pieces. Dust with flour and roll each piece into a thick round, then cut each round in half. Fold each half into a cone and brush the seam with water to prepare the seal.

5. Fill the cone with a spoonful of filling and then dampen the top edge and press to seal firmly.

6. In a deep-sided, heavy pot, heat oil until shimmering. Fry samosas a few at a time, turning occasionally, for 3-4 minutes or until golden brown. Drain on paper towels.

7. Serve hot with chutney.

CHOCOLATE CAKE

INGREDIENTS

1½ cups (185g, 6oz) plain flour

1 cup (220g, 8oz) white sugar

¼ cup (30g, 1oz) cocoa

1 tsp baking soda

½ tsp salt

1/3 cup (80ml, 3fl oz) vegetable oil

1 tsp vanilla essence

1 tsp white vinegar

1 cup (250ml, 8fl oz) water

Mixed berries, to serve

METHOD

1. Preheat oven to 180°C (350°F, Gas Mark 4). Lightly grease a 23cm (9 in) x 13cm (5 in) cake tin.

2. Sift together flour, sugar, cocoa, baking soda and salt over a bowl. Add the oil, vanilla, vinegar and water. Mix together until smooth.

3. Pour into prepared pan and bake in oven for 45 minutes. Remove from oven and allow to cool.

4. Serve with mixed berries.

CARROT-BANANA NUTBREAD

INGREDIENTS

1 cup (90g, 3oz) rolled oats

1 cup (125g, 4oz) flour, sifted

⅔ cup (140g, 5oz) sugar

1½ tsps baking powder

1 tsp bicarbonate of soda

¼ tsp salt

½ tsp cinnamon

½ tsp ground ginger

¼ cup (30g, 1oz) walnuts, coarsely chopped

¼ cup (30g, 1oz) pecans, coarsely chopped

1 egg, beaten

2 ripe bananas

2 carrots, grated

100g (3½oz) butter, melted

2 tbsps peanut butter

1 tsp vanilla

1 tbsp lemon juice

METHOD

1. Preheat oven to 180°C (350°F, Gas Mark 4) and line a 20 x 10 x 7cm (8 x 4 x 3in) loaf tin with greaseproof paper.

2. Combine dry ingredients and nuts in a bowl. Set aside.

3. Place egg, bananas, carrots, melted butter, peanut butter, vanilla and lemon juice in a large bowl and mix until well combined.

4. Add wet ingredients to dry ingredients and stir until just combined.

5. Scrape into tin and smooth the surface with a spatula. Top with pecan halves.

6. Bake for 50 minutes or until a skewer inserted in the centre comes out clean.

SERVES 10 ★ PREP 40min ★ COOK 20min

MATCHA GREEN TEA BROWNIE

INGREDIENTS

250g (9oz) unsalted butter

1½ cup (235g, 8oz) white chocolate chips

2 eggs

¼ cup (30g, 1oz) matcha green tea powder

1 cup (125g, 4oz) flour

½ tsp almond extract

¼ tsp vanilla extract

½ cup (60g, 2oz) almond slices

Icing

120g (4oz) white chocolate, grated

2 tbsps water

100g (3½oz) icing sugar (optional)

1 tsp vanilla essence

METHOD

1. Preheat oven to 180°C (350°F, Gas Mark 4). Grease and flour a baking tin.

2. Place the the butter and 1 cup of the white chocolate chips in a small heatproof bowl, set over a pan of simmering water. Cook, stirring, for until melted and smooth.

3. Pour melted chocolate into the bowl of a stand mixer. Allow to cool for 2-3 minutes then add eggs and matcha powder to the bowl and beat on low until combined.

4. Add flour, almond and vanilla extract and mix until just incorporated. Fold in almonds and white chocolate chips.

5. Pour batter into prepared pan and spread evenly with a spatula.

6. Place in the oven and bake for 20 minutes until firm to the touch.

7. Remove from the oven and place tin on a wire rack to cool.

8. Melt the white chocolate and water in a saucepan over a low heat. Sift in the icing sugar, if using, and add vanilla essence. Stir until completely dissolved.

9. When still warm, scrape icing into a piping bag, or snap lock bag with the corner removed, and pipe on top of the brownies in diagonal lines.

PEANUT BUTTER CACAO BLISS BALLS

INGREDIENTS

14 pitted dates

1 tbsp cacao powder (or cocoa powder)

2 tsp flax seeds

2 tsp sesame seeds

2 tbsps peanut butter

¾ cup (90g, 3oz) raw almonds

1 tbsp agave syrup (or honey)

METHOD

1. Place the dates, cacao powder, linseeds, sesame seeds and peanut butter into a food processor, and blend until the mixture resembles a paste.

2. Add the almonds and pulse in bursts until a coarse and slightly sticky consistency is achieved. If mixture is too dry, add agave syrup and pulse. Keep adding more syrup, if needed, to reach a good consistency for rolling.

3. Use your hands to roll the mixture into balls.

4. Eat immediately or store in an airtight container in the fridge for up to one week.

CHOCOLATE AND BEETROOT MUFFINS

INGREDIENTS

2 tbs flaxseed meal

5 tbsps water

1 cup (165g, 6oz) roast beetroot puree

¼ cup (60ml, 2fl oz) melted coconut oil

¼ cup (60ml, 2fl oz) maple syrup

1 cup (155g, 5oz) coconut sugar

1½ tsp bicarbonate of soda

¼ tsp sea salt

¼ cup (60ml, 2fl oz) unsweetened almond milk

½ cup (60g, 2oz) unsweetened cocoa powder

1 ⅓ cups (165g, 5½ oz) wholemeal flour (or plain)

METHOD

1. Preheat oven to 190°C (375°F, Gas Mark 5) and line 12 muffin cups with paper cases.

2. Combine flaxseed meal and water and allow to soak for 5 minutes.

3. Add beetroot puree, coconut oil, maple syrup, coconut sugar, bicarb and salt and mix well.

4. Add almond milk and whisk.

5. Add cocoa powder and flour. Mix until combined.

6. Divide evenly among muffin cups.

7. Bake for 20 minutes, until cake tester comes out clean from centre.

8. Allow to cool slightly on a wire rack before serving.

CASHEW BANANA OAT BARS

INGREDIENTS

1½ cup (130g, 4½oz)
rolled oats, ground
to a flour

½ cup (60g, 2oz) oat bran

½ cup (40g, 1½oz)
desiccated coconut

½ cup (60g, 2oz)
cashews, chopped finely

½ tsp salt

½ cup (115g, 4oz)
 cashew butter

¼ cup (60ml, 2fl oz)
brown rice syrup

1 small ripe banana,
mashed

1tbsp coconut oil

Handful cashews,
to garnish

METHOD

1. Mix together the rolled oats, oat bran, desicated coconut, chopped cashews and sea salt.

2. Over a low-medium heat, gently melt cashew butter, coconut oil and brown rice syrup until mixed well. Stir through mashed banana.

3. Remove from heat when starting to bubble and add to dry ingredients.

4. Mix wet and dry ingredients until well combined.

5. Transfer mixture to a lined baking dish. Press into dish and smooth top.

6. Refrigerate for at least 4 hours.

7. When set, remove from baking dish and cut into bars.

8. Garnish with whole cashews.

COCONUT BLUEBERRY CHIA SEED PUDDING

INGREDIENTS

1 cup (250ml, 8fl oz) coconut milk

3 tbsps chia seeds

2 tbsps honey or maple syrup

½ tsp vanilla extract

1½ cups (150g, 5oz) fresh blueberries

Black sesame seeds, to decorate

METHOD

1. In a jar or mixing bowl, combine coconut milk, chia seeds, honey and vanilla .

2. Chill in fridge for 15 minutes.

3. After 15 minutes, take out and stir through ingredients then return to fridge for at least 2 hours.

4. Remove from fridge and divide mixture evenly to spoon into serving glasses.

5. Fill glass with chia pudding and serve topped with blueberries.

6. Decorate with a sprinkle of black sesame seeds, if desired.

BLACKCURRANT AND LEMON FROZEN YOGHURT

INGREDIENTS

2 cups (500ml, 1pt) Greek yoghurt

¼ cup (55g, 2oz) sugar

2 tsp vanilla extract

5 cups (500g, 1lb 2oz) fresh or frozen blackcurrants

¼ cup (90g, 3oz) honey

1 tsp lemon zest

1 tbsp lemon juice

METHOD

1. Combine yoghurt, sugar and vanilla and refrigerate for 1 hour.

2. Mash together blackcurrants, honey, lemon zest and lemon juice. Refrigerate for 1 hour.

3. Combine yoghurt mixture with blackcurrant mixture in a food processor and return to freezer. Leave to set.

4. Remove from freezer 10 minutes before serving.

SERVES 12 ★ PREP 25min ★ COOK TIME 20min

PUMPKIN CHOCOLATE CHIP MUFFINS

INGREDIENTS

2 cups (250g, 8oz) plain flour

½ cup (40g, 1½ oz) oats (reserve 2 tbsps for garnish)

2 tsps baking powder

1 tsp cinnamon

½ tsp ground ginger

¼ tsp nutmeg

¼ tsp ground cloves

½ tsp salt

6 tbsps butter

1 ⅓ cup (205g, 7oz) light brown sugar

2 large eggs

1⅓ (300g, 10oz) pumpkin, boiled and puréed

1 tsp vanilla extract

¾ cup (60g, 2oz) chocolate chips (reserve 1 tbsp for garnish)

1 tbsp poppy seeds

METHOD

1. Preheat oven to 180°C (350°F, Gas Mark 4). Line a 12-hole muffin tray with paper cases.

2. In a medium bowl, combine flour, oats, baking powder, cinnamon, ginger, nutmeg, cloves and salt. Set aside.

3. Using an electric mixer on high speed, cream together butter and sugar until light and fluffy. Add the eggs, one at a time, beating after each addition.

4. Add the pumpkin purée and vanilla extract and mix to combine. Stir in the dry ingredients and the chocolate chips, mixing until just combined. Spoon the batter into the prepared paper cases so they are two thirds of the way full. Sprinkle over the reserved oats and chocolate chips and the poppy seeds.

5. Place in oven and bake for 20 minutes. The muffins are done when the tops looked cracked and golden brown and a skewer inserted in the centre comes out clean.

6. Remove from the oven, allow to stand for 5 minutes before cooling completely on a wire rack.

CHOCOLATE RICE PUDDING

INGREDIENTS

175g (6oz) dark chocolate, coarsely chopped

1 cup (155g, 4oz) short grain rice

5 cups (1.25L, 42fl oz) water

1/3 cup (50g, 2oz) brown sugar

3/4 cup (185ml, 6fl oz) vanilla almond milk

1 tbsp cornflour

Fresh cream, and cinnamon to serve

METHOD

1. Gently melt chocolate in a bowl over a saucepan of simmering water. Stir until smooth and fully melted. Remove from heat. Set aside.

2. Rinse and strain rice. Transfer to a saucepan and add water. Bring to the boil. Reduce heat to low and simmer for 15 minutes, until rice is soft and liquid thickens.

3. Add sugar, melted chocolate, almond milk and cornflour to the rice and stir through. Simmer for 5 minutes.

4. Remove from heat and let sit for 45 minutes.

5. Spoon into serving glass. Serve with cream and a sprinkle of cinnamon.

SERVES 12 ★ PREP 10MIN ★ COOK TIME 20MIN

BANANA MUFFINS

INGREDIENTS

1¾ cups (215g, 7oz) plain flour

½ tsp baking powder

1 tsp bicarb soda

½ tsp nutmeg

½ tsp salt

3 ripe bananas, mashed

¾ cup (165g, 6oz) caster sugar

1 egg

80g (3oz) butter, melted

METHOD

1. Preheat oven to 180°C (350°F, Gas Mark 4) and line a 12-hole muffin tray with paper cases.

2. Sift together the flour, baking powder, bicarb soda, nutmeg and salt in a medium mixing bowl. Set aside.

3. Combine mashed bananas, sugar, egg and melted butter in a large mixing bowl. Gradually fold in dry ingredient mix, and combine with a metal spoon until smooth. Spoon into paper cases, filling two thirds full with batter.

4. Place in the oven and bake for 20 minutes, or until the muffins are brown on top and a skewer inserted in the centre comes out clean.

5. Remove from the oven, allow to stand for 5 minutes before cooling completely on a wire rack.

SERVES 6 ★ PREP 40MIN (PLUS CHILLING) ★ COOK TIME 55MIN

PECAN PIE

INGREDIENTS

Shortcrust pastry

1¾ cups (215g, 7oz)
plain flour, sifted

Pinch of salt

125g (4oz) chilled butter,
chopped

1 egg, lightly beaten

1 tbsp iced water

Filling

50g (2oz) butter,
chopped

1 cup (155g, 5oz)
brown sugar

⅔ cup (230g, 8oz)
golden syrup

3 eggs, beaten

1 tsp vanilla extract

2 cups (250g, 8oz)
pecans, roughly chopped

4 pecan halves, to
decorate

METHOD

1. Combine flour and salt in a large bowl. Add butter and rub into flour mixture using fingertips until fine breadcrumbs form. Make a well in centre of flour mixture. Combine egg and water in a small bowl, then pour into well. Using a round-bladed knife, or your hands, stir until mixture just forms a dough.

2. Turn out onto a floured surface and shape into a disc. Wrap in plastic wrap and chill in fridge for 30 minutes.

3. Preheat oven to 200°C (390°F, Gas Mark 6) and prepare a round tart tin.

4. Place dough on a floured work surface and roll out to size, using the base of the dish as a guide. Line tin with pastry using the rolling pin to fold over the dish. Trim and discard excess pastry. Cover and refrigerate for 15 minutes.

5. Blind bake for 20 minutes or until pastry is golden. Remove weights and paper. Reduce oven to 175°C (350°F, Gas Mark 4).

6. Place butter, sugar and golden syrup in a small saucepan over low–medium heat. Cook for 5 minutes, stirring constantly, until butter melts and mixture is smooth. Remove from heat and set aside to cool slightly. Add eggs and vanilla, and whisk to combine. Add chopped nuts and stir well to combine.

7. Add filling into the pastry base and smooth over with a spatula. Press pecan halves in the centre to decorate.

8. Place dish on a tray and bake for 35 minutes or until filling is browned and firm to the touch. Remove from oven and cool in dish.

CASHEW COCONUT BUTTER

INGREDIENTS

1½ cups (185g, 6oz)
toasted cashews

¼ cup (20g, ¾ oz)
coconut chips

1 tsp coconut oil

½ tsp salt

METHOD

1. In a food processor, blend cashews for 5 minutes,
   until smooth and creamy.

2. Add coconut chips, coconut oil and salt, to taste,
   and continue to blend until combined.

3. Place in a sterilised jar.

4. Spread on bread or toast, to serve.

   Note: Can be kept at room temperature for 2 weeks,
   or in the fridge for up to 3 months.

ZUCCHINI BREAD

INGREDIENTS

3 cups (375g, 12oz)
plain flour

2 tsps baking powder

¼ tsp bicarbonate of soda

2 tsps cinnamon

¼ tsp nutmeg

1 tsp salt

2 eggs

1 cup (220g, 8oz) sugar

½ cup (80g, 3oz) brown
sugar, packed

¾ cup (185ml, 6fl oz)
olive oil

2 tsps vanilla extract

2-3 zucchini, grated
and squeezed of excess
moisture

METHOD

1. Heat the oven to 180°C (350°F, Gas Mark 4). Grease and line two 20 x 10 x 7cm (8 x 4 x 3in) loaf tins.

2. Combine the flour, baking powder, bicarb soda, and spices in a large mixing bowl.

3. In a separate bowl, whisk together the eggs, sugars, olive oil, and vanilla extract.

4. Stir the zucchini into the flour mixture. Pour the wet mixture over the top. Gently stir and fold until flour is just fully combined. Divide the batter between the two loaf pans.

5. Place in the oven and bake for 45 minutes, until golden brown and a skewer inserted in the centre comes out clean.

6. Remove from oven and allow to cool in tin for 5 minutes and then turn onto a wire rack to cool completely.

INDEX

First Published in 2016 by Herron Book Distributors Pty Ltd
14 Manton St
Morningside
QLD 4170
www.herronbooks.com

Custom book production by Captain Honey Pty Ltd
12 Station St
Bangalow
NSW 2479
www.captainhoney.com.au

Cataloguing-in-Publication. A catalogue record for this book is
available from the National Library of Australia

ISBN 978-0-947163-16-7

All images used under license from Shutterstock.com
Printed and bound in China by 1010 Printing International Limited

5 4 3 2   19 20

NOTES FOR THE READER

Preparation, cooking times and serving sizes vary according to
the skill, agility and appetite of the cook and should be used as a
guide only.

All reasonable efforts have been made to ensure the accuracy of
the content in this book. Information in this book is not intended
as a substitute for medical advice. The author and publisher
cannot and do not accept any legal duty of care or responsibility
in relation to the content in this book, and disclaim any liabilities
relating to its use.